St. Teresa of Ávila

AND

THE OUR FATHER

A HAGIOS SCRIPTURE STUDY

Kristina Romero with Fr. Jeffrey Kirby

Our Sunday Visitor
Huntington, Indiana

Nihil Obstat
Msgr. Michael Heintz, Ph.D.
Censor Librorum

Imprimatur
Kevin C. Rhoades
Bishop of Fort Wayne-South Bend
September 11, 2025

The *Nihil Obstat* and *Imprimatur* are official declarations that a book is free from doctrinal or moral error. It is not implied that those who have granted the *Nihil Obstat* and *Imprimatur* agree with the contents, opinions, or statements expressed.

31 30 29 28 27 26   1 2 3 4 5 6 7 8 9

Our Sunday Visitor Publishing Division
Our Sunday Visitor, Inc.
200 Noll Plaza
Huntington, IN 46750
www.osv.com
1-800-348-2440

ISBN: 978-1-63966-379-8 (Inventory No. T3005)
1. RELIGION—Biblical Studies—New Testament—Jesus, the Gospels & Acts.
2. RELIGION—Christianity—Saints & Sainthood.
3. RELIGION—Christianity—Catholic.

eISBN: 978-1-63966-380-4
LCCN: 2025946168

Cover and interior design: Kristina Romero, Romero Media
Cover and interior art: Kristina Romero, Romero Media, and Adobestock

PRINTED IN THE UNITED STATES OF AMERICA

Contents

Image: A copy of St. Teresa of Ávila's writings

FOREWORD

The Sacred Scriptures are the revealed word of God. As believers, we are invited every day to read, pray, study, and do our best to plumb the depths of this powerful revelation that has been given to us.

Such a task can seem overwhelming, which is why it's such a great blessing and encouragement when resources come along that can help us engage with and learn from the Sacred Scriptures. Kristina Romeo offers us such a resource. In this study, she walks us through the beauty of the Lord's Prayer.

The Lord's Prayer was given to us by the Lord Jesus himself. It was provided as a response to a request by his disciples that he teach us how to pray. It directs us in our prayer to God and shapes how we speak and listen to him. The Lord's Prayer is the synthesis of the entire Gospel. It shows us how profoundly God loves us and how eager he is to care for us.

Each of the six petitions of the Lord's Prayer reflects the life-changing truths given to us by Jesus Christ. Each of the six chapters of this book dives into one of the six petitions of the Lord's Prayer. Unpacking each part — Secret, Holy Father, Kingdom, Bread, Forgiven, and Trial — this study offers us six small schools of instruction on the Lord's Prayer and the spiritual life.

Yet this book does not present the truths of the Lord's Prayer by itself. Instead, it brings in teachings of the spiritual master, St. Teresa of Ávila, to help us understand this prayer in its fullness.

There is no better guide to the Sacred Scripture than the saints. They are the men and women who encountered God and came to truly know him during their lives on earth. The teachings of the saints, especially those in the mystical tradition, are some of our best witnesses and teachers in the mystery and ways of God. And so, looking to Saint Teresa for guidance in this exposition on the Lord's Prayer will lead us to the rich fountain of divine wisdom.

Each chapter of this study offers us various perspectives on the same truth. This approach allows us to see and experience the different dimensions of what God is revealing to us. Each chapter is developed, encapsulated, and crowned by a lesson based on the saintly life and writings of Saint Teresa of Ávila.

Throughout each chapter, there is a call to engage with the word of God. Each chapter then concludes with an invitation to rest and reflect on a specific petition of the Lord's Prayer.

There are many ways to study the Sacred Scriptures, just as there are many ways to approach the Lord's Prayer. This book presents a way that welcomes the insight of the early Fathers of the Church and engages the keen spiritual wisdom of the Doctor of Prayer herself, Saint Teresa of Ávila. It is a way of studying the Sacred Scriptures that places them in the midst of holiness and in the company of a great cloud of witnesses (Heb 12:1–2).

I encourage you to let the holy ones direct you in your encounter with the word of God as you walk through the Lord's Prayer and come to a greater awareness of God's love and care for you.

Fr. Jeffrey Kirby, S.T.D.

Author, *Thy Kingdom Come: Living the Lord's Prayer in Everyday Life*

MUSIC MEDITATIONS ON THE HAGIOS STUDY APP

Visit your app store to download the free Hagios Study app. Inside the app are various audiovisual experiences that will enhance your journey as well as the study in digital form.

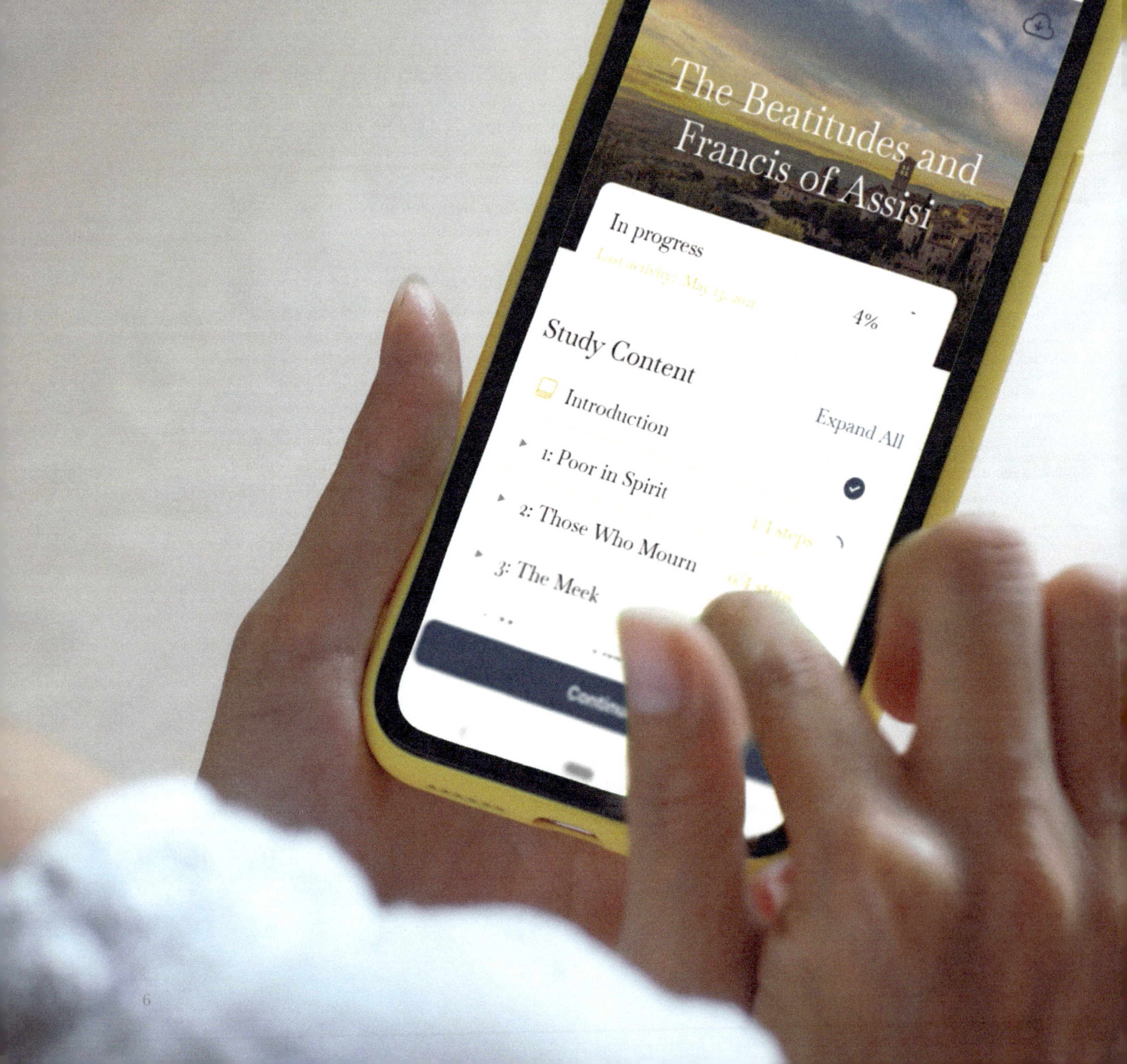

How to use this study

This six-week study can be used for small group study or personal study. Each week is broken up into four sections following the *lectio divina* method (Latin for "divine reading"). Below are the features of a Hagios Study that will enhance your journey through Scripture.

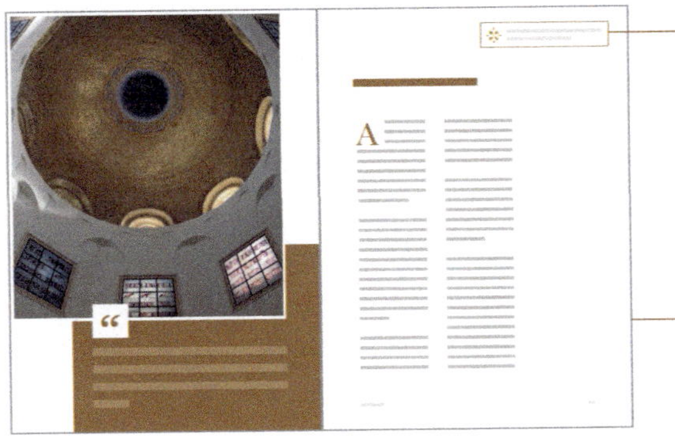

APP PROMPT

These prompts encourage you to visit our free mobile app to enhance your journey through this study. Use the QR code to download the app or visit hagios.study/osv.

READ, REFLECT, RESPOND, REST

Each section of this book follows the ancient *lectio divina* method for Scripture study. You can do all four sections in one day or break them up over a week.

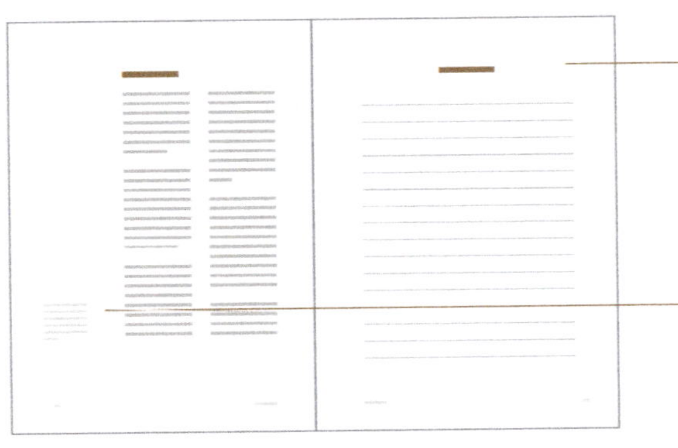

JOURNAL

This study encourages journaling and note-taking. The "Reflect Notes" sections are for you to record your thoughts and observations.

SIDEBAR

The sidebars are specifically designed for note-taking. Use this space to highlight verses, journal thoughts, or add comments.

QUESTIONS

Each part of this book includes a question section meant to encourage contemplation, analysis, and reflection. These questions are also ideal for small group discussions.

Lectio Divina

Each chapter of this study is divided into four sections, each section focusing on one step in the ancient monastic practice of *lectio divina*, Latin for "divine reading." This prayerful method of reading Scripture was taught by several saints in the early Church, including especially St. Benedict of Nursia, who established it as part of his Rule for his monks. The practice was later fleshed out into a four-step process by the Carthusian monk Guigo II in the twelfth century. The purpose of the format for *lectio divina* is to help us enter into a conversation with God. The goal is to make Scripture come alive and provide a way for you to connect with God's word on a level that is both personal and convicting.

The format consists of four steps: reading, reflecting, responding, and resting. In each step, we seek to be guided by the Holy Spirit. There's plenty of flexibility in how you choose to approach each chapter: You can do one section a day or all four in one day. That's up to how the Spirit is leading you.

THE LADDER OF FOUR RUNGS

Reading seeks,
meditation finds,
prayer asks,
contemplation feels. …

Reading puts as it were whole
food into your mouth;

meditation chews it and breaks
it down;

prayer finds its savour;

contemplation is the sweetness
that so delights and strengthens.

Reading is like the bark, the
shell;

meditation like the pith, the nut;

prayer is in the desiring asking;

and contemplation is in the
delight of the great sweetness.

(**Guigo II, 1140–1193**)

READ

"Reading seeks." The READ section explores the featured verses by viewing them alongside supporting verses that include shared keywords. Comparing the same words across the Greek versions of the Old and New Testaments helps us better understand the English translation and how these parallel verses give insight into the main reading. This section allows you to take in the information intellectually before you move into REFLECT. As Guigo II noted, "Reading puts as it were whole food into your mouth."

REFLECT

"Meditation finds." The REFLECT section offers short reflections from ancient Church Fathers to aid you in discovering how to apply the Scripture verses to your life. In this section, ask the Holy Spirit to reveal to you what he wants to say to you, then, if you wish, journal your notes in the space provided. This section encourages you to seek out a moment of meditation before you move on to RESPOND. Let the presented reflections give you the means to "chew it and break it down." (For even more material for meditation, you can use the experiential meditation available in the Hagios mobile app.)

RESPOND

"Prayer asks." The RESPOND section unfolds a story of response in the life of a Christian. Through the witness of a saint, you will discover how the Holy Spirit has led others and gain deeper insight into how he might be leading you to live your Christian call more fully. Studying the lives of the saints as a response to Scripture allows you to "find its savour" to determine how the Holy Spirit is leading you.

REST

"Contemplation feels." The final section, REST, brings together each of the previous three sections for a moment of final considerations. This section provides two ways for you to settle into "the sweetness that so delights and strengthens." REST will encourage you to digest all the Holy Spirit has revealed to you throughout the week as you move along your journey through the study. (If you want a more immersive experience, begin this section by listening to a contemporary praise song on the mobile app while meditating on the verses from the READ section.)

> *And whenever you pray, do not be like the hypocrites; for they love to stand and pray in the synagogues and at the street corners, so that they may be seen by others. Truly I tell you, they have received their reward."* (Mt 6:5)

Image: Church of the Pater Noster (Our Father) in Jerusalem, Israel

Introduction

DOWNLOAD THE FREE HAGIOS STUDY APP TO ENHANCE YOUR JOURNEY THROUGH THE STUDY

TEACH US TO PRAY

One common thread in the lives of saints is the desire for prayer and the recognition of its critical importance. A saint's prayer life can feel otherworldly and often too far removed from our own time to be relevant. The busyness of our regular, everyday lives can lead us to think that a rich prayer life isn't within our grasp.

Yet the reality is that prayer is timeless, it's for all of us, and the best prayer looks to Jesus as both example and end. St. Teresa of Ávila, a sixteenth-century Spanish nun and reformer of the Carmelite Order, has much to teach us on this point. She is a Doctor of the Church, and her teachings on prayer have earned her the title Doctor of Prayer. During her life, when people asked her about prayer (which included tangible intimacy with Christ, constant communication with the Father, and sensitivity to the Spirit), Teresa simply pointed to the prayer that Jesus taught during his Sermon on the Mount. Yes, that prayer — the one we say in every Mass, in every Rosary, and in moments of desperation when no other prayers will come: the prayer we know as the "Our Father."

In the Gospel of Luke, the disciples ask Jesus, "Teach us to pray" (11:1). The prayer he teaches them is very similar to the prayer we know so well from Matthew's Gospel. This prayer is so familiar to any Christian that you can probably recite it without even thinking about it. And since this study will focus on this prayer specifically, you can probably already recite by heart most of the verses we will explore. Is the path to a deeper prayer life, to communication and communion with God, really that simple?

Saint Teresa thought so. In fact, once she sat down to write out her reflections on the Our Father, she was surprised by how much she had to say. She wrote, "Certainly, it never entered my mind that this prayer contained so many deep secrets."[1] So don't be fooled by the simplicity of this prayer; it contains the depths of what we need to know about prayer and is, indeed, our teacher on the way to prayer.

Teresa came to know the "deep secrets" of the Lord's Prayer intimately, secrets that God instructed her to share with the world. Her writings led Pope St. Paul VI to name her the first female Doctor of the Church in 1970, the first of only four female Doctors in the Church's history. Two of Teresa's works — her *Life* and *The Way of Perfection* — will guide our study of Matthew 6:5–15.

In this six-part study, we will dive into the words of Jesus in the Gospel of Matthew as he teaches us to pray from the beautiful lakeside landscape known as the Mount of the Beatitudes. We will also visit the walled-off medieval city of Ávila, Spain, to learn about prayer from a simple, seemingly ordinary woman who had a gift of understanding that baffled the priests and bishops of her day.

TERESA'S WRITINGS

Teresa of Ávila can, at first, seem hard to understand. She was a woman of her time, who dwelt on and paid much attention to sins we often brush aside today. Meanwhile, she had experiences with Jesus that were profound, intense, and visceral — experiences that included levitations, visions, and catatonic episodes. These experiences make many of us today say, "That's a little too much for me."

Yet Teresa wanted her fellow religious sisters (and us today) to realize that these were manifestations of God's love. It's the same love he has for each of us, a love that is constantly inviting us into "sonship."

Two works of Teresa are referenced throughout this study and will guide our understanding. The first is *The Book of Her Life*. Although it contains autobiographical elements, it was not written like an autobiography. It was simply a way for her to communicate and put into words what she experienced. The book is written like a letter to her confessors, the priests from whom she sought counsel. The other work is *The Way of Perfection*. This book was a response to her fellow nuns, who asked her for guidance on how to pray. Her insights are invaluable for us today as well, whether we live in a monastery or in the world. She encouraged:

> Our primitive rule states that we must pray without ceasing. … Before I say anything about interior matters, that is, about prayer, I shall mention some things that are necessary for those who seek to follow the way of prayer. … The first of these is love for one another; the second is detachment from all created things; the third is true humility, which, even though I speak of it last, is the main practice and embraces all the others.[2]

These three virtues, love, detachment, and humility, shine forth in Saint Teresa's life and example, and we will explore each of them in turn as we move through this study.

May Christ's words, combined with the example of Saint Teresa, serve as an invitation to deepen our prayer life so that we may accept all the Lord desires to give us and all he desires to work through us.

Jesus' Ministry in Matthew

Jesus began his ministry in the region of Galilee in Northern Israel. During his ministry in Jerusalem he preached, performed miracles, and told many parables before he was crucified and then rose from the dead.

BIRTH OF JESUS
c. 4–6 BC (Mt 1)

THE BAPTISM OF JESUS
c. AD 27 (Mt 3:13–17)

TEMPTATION OF JESUS
27 (Mt 4:1–11)

JESUS CALLS HIS FIRST DISCIPLES
27 (Mt 4:18–22)

SERMON ON THE MOUNT (THE OUR FATHER)
27 (Mt 5–7)

MINISTRY AND HEALINGS
27–30 (Mt 8–20)

PALM SUNDAY, ENTRY INTO JERUSALEM
30 (Mt 21)

FINAL PASSOVER AND BETRAYAL
30 (Mt 26)

JESUS' CRUCIFIXION
30 (Mt 27)

JESUS' RESURRECTION
30 (Mt 28)

Teresa's Life

Teresa Sánchez de Cepeda y Ahumada was born in Ávila, Spain, during the start of the Protestant Reformation. She would go on to be a key figure in the Catholic Counter-Reformation and would become the first female Doctor of the Church.

BORN TERESA SÁNCHEZ DE CEPEDA Y AHUMADA
March 28, 1515

ATTEMPTS TO RUN AWAY WITH HER BROTHER TO BE A MARTYR
1522

TERESA'S MOTHER DIES
1529

ENTERS CARMELITE CONVENT OF THE INCARNATION IN ÁVILA
1535

NEARLY DIES FROM ILLNESS
1538–1539

EXPERIENCES CONVERSION (DURING LENT)
1554

BEGINS TO WRITE *THE BOOK OF HER LIFE*
1560

FOUNDS THE CONVENT OF ST. JOSEPH
1562

WRITES *THE INTERIOR CASTLE*
1577

DIES IN ALBA DE TORMES
October 4, 1582

Image: Church of the Pater Noster (Our Father) in Jerusalem, Israel

Scripture

MATTHEW 6:5-15

5 "And whenever you pray, do not be like the hypocrites; for they love to stand and pray in the synagogues and at the street corners, so that they may be seen by others. Truly I tell you, they have received their reward. 6 But whenever you pray, go into your room and shut the door and pray to your Father who is in secret; and your Father who sees in secret will reward you.

7 "When you are praying, do not heap up empty phrases as the Gentiles do; for they think that they will be heard because of their many words. 8 Do not be like them, for your Father knows what you need before you ask him.

9 "Pray then in this way:
Our Father in heaven,
hallowed be your name.

10 Your kingdom come.
Your will be done,
on earth as it is in heaven.

11 Give us this day our daily bread.

12 And forgive us our debts,
as we also have forgiven our debtors.

13 And do not bring us to the time of trial,
but rescue us from the evil one.

14 For if you forgive others their trespasses, your heavenly Father will also forgive you; 15 but if you do not forgive others, neither will your Father forgive your trespasses.

PATER NOSTER (OUR FATHER IN LATIN)

9 Pater Noster, qui es in caelis, sanctificetur nomen tuum.

10 Adveniat regnum tuum. Fiat voluntas tua, sicut in caelo et in terra.

11 Panem nostrum quotidianum da nobis hodie,

12 et dimitte nobis debita nostra sicut et nos dimittimus debitoribus nostris.

13 Et ne nos inducas in tentationem, sed libera nos a malo. Amen.

PADRE NUESTRO (OUR FATHER IN SPANISH)

9 Padre nuestro, que estás en el cielo. Santificado sea tu nombre.

10 Venga tu reino. Hágase tu voluntad en la tierra como en el cielo.

11 Danos hoy nuestro pan de cada día.

12 Perdona nuestras ofensas, como también nosotros perdonamos a los que nos ofenden.

13 No nos dejes caer en tentación y líbranos del mal. Amén.

Image: The walls surrounding the city of Ávila, Spain

Image: Panoramic view of Ávila, Spain

SECTION 1

Secret

"

But whenever you pray, go into your room and shut the door and pray to your Father who is in secret; and your Father who sees in secret will reward you." (Mt 6:6)

Image: The Church of the Beatitudes by the Sea of Galilee in Israel

DEEP DIVE INTO SCRIPTURE: MATTHEW 6:5-8

To study Matthew 6:5–8 in context, we will start by exploring other verses in Scripture that also speak of secret and reward. Since the New Testament was written in Greek, we've included parallel verses that use the same Greek word for secret (*kryptos*) or kingdom of heaven (*apodidōmi*). Look up and write out the verses below using your own Bible translation. Engaging in this exercise helps us understand Matthew 6:5–8 in the full context of Scripture, showing how these verses apply yesterday, today, and forever.

Word/Phrase	Verse	Write Out His Word
secret, recessed, hidden (English) *kryptos* (Greek)	Psalm 119:10–11	
	Jeremiah 23:23–24	
	Matthew 13:34–35	
reward, repay (English) *apodidōmi* (Greek)	Job 33:26	
	Romans 2:6–7	
	Revelation 22:12–13	

IN THE SECRET

Are we truly seeking the Lord in our time of prayer? It's easy to fall into the trap of saying prayers without trying to enter into deeper intimacy with God through our prayer. Remember that the people who cried "Crucify him!" on Good Friday were largely faithful Jews who studied the law and recited their prayers. It's not enough merely to pray; we need to look to Jesus to learn how to pray and avoid "babbling" — as the Greek translates "anxiously using empty words."

Within the great Sermon on the Mount, recorded in Matthew chapters 5–7, Jesus clarifies that prayer is an interior practice, a secret expression. It is a place where we meet with God, where we learn who God is and who we are.

***kryptos* (Greek) — secret, recessed, hidden**

The Greek verb used for "secret," *kryptos* (pronounced kroop-tos), is where we get the words crypt and cryptography (the study of breaking secret codes).[1] Kryptos is the first step to a deeper prayer life.

In the Old Testament, the faithful hid to escape the evil forces of the world, as David hid from Saul after his anointing as king in 1 Samuel. The hidden place becomes a refuge and a place to encounter the omnipotent God.

The psalmist sings: "With my whole heart I seek you; do not let me stray from your commandments. I treasure (*kryptos*) your word in my heart, so that I may not sin against you" (Ps 119:10–11).

In the hidden and secret places, we cherish the most precious things. The Prophet Jeremiah encourages Israel with the Lord's own words: "Am I a God near by, says the LORD, and not a God far off? Who can hide in secret (*kryptos*) places so that I cannot see them? says the LORD. Do I not fill heaven and earth? says the LORD" (Jer 23:23–24).

The secret is an opportunity for more. For it is in the interior of our hearts that God can speak to us and reveal to us his own nature.

In Deuteronomy 29:29, we read: "The secret (*kryptos*) things belong to the LORD our God, but the revealed things belong to us and to our children forever, to observe all the words of this law."

Understanding the hidden, or secret, ways of God is challenging; it forces us to think. It's why Jesus often spoke in parables. The truth Jesus revealed in these parables was precious. Through the ancient, Semitic way of storytelling he found a new way to teach us by helping us to reach for the hidden wisdom of God.

"Jesus told the crowds all these things in parables; without a parable he told them nothing. This was to fulfill what had been spoken through the prophet: 'I will open my mouth to speak in parables; I will proclaim what has been hidden (*kryptos*) from the foundation of the world'" (Mt 13:34–35).

What a gift the words of Jesus become when we see him as our God, reaching out to us and inviting us to learn the secrets of his heart.

TO BE REWARDED

The Sermon on the Mount was indeed the wisdom of God revealed to us, and in the Gospel of Matthew, Jesus teaches us the Our Father in the greater context of this sermon. In the beginning of Matthew chapter 5, Jesus lists the Beatitudes, the promise of divine acceptance toward those who are poor in spirit, the meek, the humble, the peacemakers, and those seeking righteousness. So then, what do we make of the reference to reward in our verses today about those who seek the Lord in the secret?

***apodidōmi* (Greek) — repay, give away, restore**

The verb used for "reward" is *apodidōmi* (pronounced ap-od-eed'-o-mee), which also means to pay, repay, give away, or restore. It is repeatedly used in the Old Testament as an expression of fulfilled vows.[2]

In the story of Job, even as he loses everything, Job remains faithful, though he does not understand his sufferings. We read, "Then he prays to God, and is accepted by him, he comes into his presence with joy, and God repays [*apodidōmi*] him for his righteousness" (Jb 33:26).

In the New Testament, we encounter this same word in the Gospel of Luke, when Jesus tells the disciples to give back to Caesar what is Caesar's: "He said to them, 'Then give [*apodidōmi*] to the emperor the things that are the emperor's, and to God the things that are God's'" (Lk 20:25).

Drawing a parallel to repayment, we can hear Jesus implying that (among other things) seeking out an attentive and interior life of prayer is paying to God what is God's, an action for which the Lord will reward us.

In Romans 2:6–7, Paul explains, "For he will repay [*apodidōmi*] according to each one's deeds: to those who by patiently doing good seek for glory and honor and immortality, he will give eternal life."

In Revelation Jesus promises, "See, I am coming soon; my reward is with me, to repay [*apodidōmi*] according to everyone's work. I am the Alpha and the Omega, the first and the last, the beginning and the end" (Rv 22:12–13).

In our verses for this week, Jesus sets the stage for the prayer he is about to teach. The first step is to seek the Father internally, in secret, just you and the Lord. Jesus also explains that this type of prayer vastly differs from what his disciples have seen or experienced. If they desire rewards from the Lord, they must follow and pray as he teaches.

As seen in the Old Testament, everything we do is known by God. Nothing we ever do is secret. But to know the Lord's ways we must seek him in the remote place of our hearts. Therefore, when we draw near to the Lord in secret, we strengthen our relationship with him so he can make known his heart and his will to us, and he will repay, according to his will.

Reflect

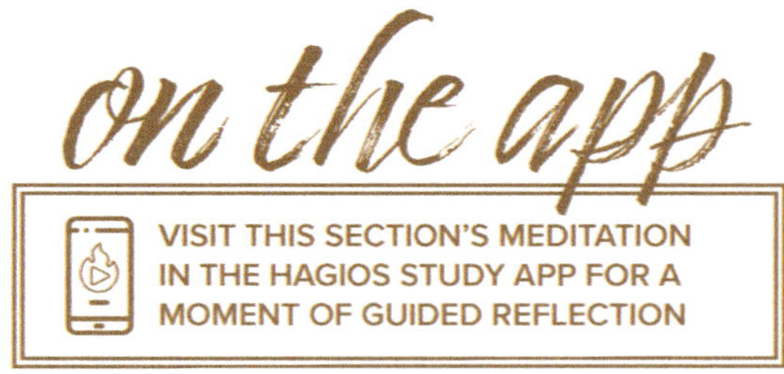

REFLECTION FROM EARLY CHURCH FATHERS

"Out of deeps call upon God, for it is said, Out of the depths have I cried to you, O Lord. From beneath, out of the heart, draw forth a voice, make your prayer a mystery. … Yes, for you are joined to the choirs of angels, and art in communion with archangels, and art singing with the seraphim. And all these tribes show forth much goodly order, singing with great awe that mystical strain, and their sacred hymns to God, the King of all. With these then mingle yourself, when you are praying, and emulate their mystical order. For not unto men are you praying, but to God, who is everywhere present, who hears even before the voice, who knows the secrets of the mind."

— St. John Chrysostom, *Homily XIX, Homilies on the Gospel of Saint Matthew;* AD 387[3]

"In order therefore that we, withdrawing far from these disgraceful ways, and escaping from the snares to which they are exposed who seek to please men, may offer to God prayer, holy and blameless and undefiled, Christ made himself our example, by going apart from those who were with him, and praying alone. For it was right that our head and teacher in every good and useful deed should be no other than he who is first among all, and receives the prayers of all, and with God the Father bestows on those who ask him whatsoever they require. …

For as the wise Paul wrote to us, 'We know not what to pray for as we ought.' Let us therefore draw near to Christ, the Giver of wisdom, and say, 'Teach us to pray.' Let us be like the holy apostles, who above all other things asked of him this profitable and saving lesson."

— St. Cyril of Alexandria[4]

As you ponder these verses, journal your thoughts in the space provided. Reflect on the Scripture passage (and subsequent supporting passages) from "Read." Is there a word or phrase that especially stands out to you? What do these verses say to you? What is the Holy Spirit showing you in these Scripture passages?

SECRET

Image: A re-creation of Teresa's room in the Convent of St. Joseph, Ávila, Spain

Respond

In this section, we will review Teresa's response to God's word. May she serve as an example as you seek out how the Holy Spirit is prompting you to respond.

THE SECRET EXPOSED

The lives of the saints reveal God's truth to us. Through their unique examples, we learn something of who God is and who we are meant to be.

St. Teresa of Ávila's example and teachings make it easier for us to understand the heavenly mysteries of prayer and what it means to have an authentic prayer life. Teresa lived during a challenging time of unrest and change in the Church, dealing with the upheavals caused by the Protestant Reformation. Remarkably, Saint Teresa had a profound impact on the Church despite having no formal theological education and spending most of her life within the radius of a small town in Spain.

Looking at Teresa and her life as a response to the prayer that Jesus taught, we begin our narrative when she was well into her sixties, when her private and secret moments with the Lord became front-page news of the Spanish Catholic post-Reformation world.

Before describing the context of her life, we must consider her unique and special character. Had Teresa lived in our time, she would have been offered her own reality television show — not because she would have wanted it but because of her attractive personality.

Before her religious life and even during it, Teresa was very popular, affable, and likable. This remained true even as she assumed the role of superior in the monasteries she founded .So, it's safe to say that today she may have had her own podcast or YouTube channel, because her priests and others would have begged her for it.

But a public life would not have been her desire. Teresa loved the secret, hidden life. Despite being called to lead reforms in her religious order, she responded well to Jesus' call in Matthew 6:6 to seek the interior life away from the world in order to encounter God.

By the time she was sixty years old, in 1575, Teresa was twenty years into receiving mystical "special favors" from the Lord. Historians classify her as a mystic, which can be a tricky word. Mystics are best described as those who experience on earth what we will all experience in heaven. And that she did.

In sixteenth-century Spain, mysticism was considered a dangerous gift. For various reasons, people were obsessed with the otherworldly and the supernatural. Because of this fascination, many "false prophets" rose to popularity, attracting followers for financial, political, and popular gain. Most notable was a woman named Magdalena de la Cruz, a Spanish Franciscan nun who faked the stigmata and other miracles. She eventually confessed to a relationship with the Devil and was sentenced to life imprisonment in a convent. Teresa would have known this story well and, because of it, knew that her own remarkable experiences would draw suspicion — and possibly worse.

Also, during Teresa's life, the Spanish Inquisition was formed to combat heresy, apostasy, blasphemy, and witchcraft. The Inquisition created a climate in which an honest nun would have been afraid to experience, much less proclaim, a profoundly personal and mystical relationship with Jesus like Teresa did.

Teresa valued obedience highly and trusted her experiences to her priests to help better discern whether they were from God. The challenge for Teresa was that most of what she shared baffled her confessors.

When questioned about Teresa, one priest-confessor pointed to a large stack of books, stating, "I have read all of these in an attempt to understand her."[5] But it was not just her confessors who were confused by her mystical life. Her fellow sisters witnessed unexplainable events such as levitations and her overwhelming bodily exhibitions of paralysis and ecstasy.

Eventually, her priests instructed her to write down all that had happened in her life, to share some of the secrets of her life with the Lord. Teresa felt this was an impossible task, and would have preferred writing about her sins. Ever faithful and obedient, however, she wrote her *Life*, or what we now call *The Book of Her Life*. In doing so, her intense interior prayer life was casually and sometimes cruelly shared with others.

When the princess of Éboli heard of Teresa's secret book, she insisted on reading it. Since the princess had made many financial donations to help fund Teresa's Discalced Carmelite monasteries, Teresa relented. The woman, however, was not careful with the document, which resulted in much gossip about Teresa and accusations made to the Inquisition. But what was Teresa's secret?

Teresa would gladly explain it: simple prayer, readily available to anyone. In her book *The Way of Perfection*, she wrote to her fellow nuns on prayer in hopes that they also would taste this amazing intimacy with God. Teresa framed prayer as requiring three things: detachment, humility, and love of neighbor. All things, she felt, could be found in praying the words of the Our Father, whether verbally or mentally.

She wrote, "For mental prayer in my opinion is nothing else than an intimate sharing between friends; it means taking time frequently to be alone with him who we know loves us."[6]

Ten years later her second book *The Interior Castle* again spoke about this secret interior life of prayer and how one can move through the different rooms of the soul to connect deeply with Jesus. "Each one of us has a soul, but since we do not prize souls as is deserved by creatures made in the image of God we do not understand the deep secrets that lie in them."[7]

It should not have, but in the difficult environment of the Inquisition, Teresa's pursuit of a deep connection with Jesus aroused suspicion. She was never afraid of the Inquisition, though. In fact, she was more fearful of being in error and would have likely brought herself before their inspection if she felt she was being deceived, or worse, deceiving others. Teresa only cared what God thought about her and desired to keep close to him in the secret place. "I fear those who have such great fear of the devil more than I do the devil himself, for he can't do anything to me. Whereas these others, especially if they are confessors, cause severe disturbance."[8]

In an attempt to help her, some of her confessors ordered her not to pray alone out of fear she was being attacked by the Devil. She writes: "My confessor told me that they all came to the decision that my experience was from the devil, that I shouldn't receive Communion so often, and that I should try to distract myself in such a way that I would not be alone. I was extremely fearful, as I said; and my heart trouble added to my fear, for I didn't very often dare remain in a room alone during the daytime."[9]

Although often misguided, her confessors were wise in requiring that she write everything down. We have all these beautiful writings about her secret encounters thanks to the culture of suspicion in which she lived. The Inquisition never brought Teresa to trial, but she suffered through deep scrutiny and a constant demand that her secret life be exposed and made public.

Through it all, in his love, the Lord continued to meet her in prayer in wild and overwhelming ways.

Teresa has a beautiful example of how she knew that her secret times with the Lord were of his design, and not evil, because of the fruit they left behind. She writes:

> I told them once that if they were to tell me that a person whom I knew very well and with whom I had just finished speaking were not that person, but that I had imagined it, I would without doubt, as they knew, believe what they said rather than what I had seen. But if this person were to leave me some jewels, and they were left in my hands as tokens of great love, I would not believe what they said, even though I desired, because I hadn't had any jewels before and was poor, whereas now I found that I was rich. I was able to show them these jewels because all who knew me saw clearly that my soul was changed.[10]

The overzealous scrutiny of Teresa has been our gain. We will partake in the favors she experienced as we make our way through her life as well as her private revelations on the Our Father in this study. We'll realize how the prayer that Jesus taught is perfectly crafted to bring us into deeper union with God if we submit as Teresa instructs, in detachment, humility, and love of neighbor.

Writing on the Our Father in *The Way of Perfection*, she says: "And it is good for us to consider that he taught this prayer to each of us and that he is showing it to us; the teacher is never so far from his pupil that he has to shout, but he is very close. I want you to understand that it is good for you, if you are to recite the Our Father well, to remain at the side of the Master who taught this prayer to you."[11]

For Teresa, prayer was all about turning inward, closing the door of the soul, and meeting God there. In all her writings and through the example of her life, Teresa invites us into the secret interior of her prayer life; she is eager to show us how to encounter the Heavenly Father.

DISCUSSION QUESTIONS

1.What was the culture like in Teresa's time? How are things different today? How are they similar?

2. Use your imagination to ponder how Teresa felt, seeking to grow in intimacy with the Lord while living under such suspicion. How would that feel?

3. How did Teresa view prayer? What three things does she say you need in order to pray well?

4. Have you ever had something secret (and sacred to you) thoughtlessly shared with others? What was that experience like?

5. How can you help your prayer life become more intimate, quiet, and inward?

6. Have you ever been in a season where it was challenging for you to pray? How did you respond?

"I have gone astray like a lost sheep; seek out your servant, for I do not forget your commandments."

(PS 119:176)

Image: A statue of Saint Teresa of Jesus outside the walls of Ávila, Spain

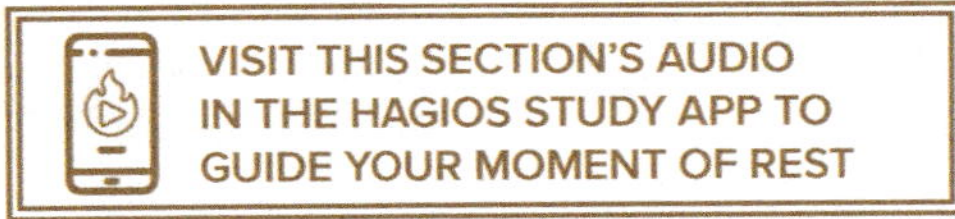

Below is a poem from Teresa of Ávila about God asking us to find him within our soul. Use this poem in a time of prayer and reflection. As you finish this part of the study, visit the Hagios Study mobile app for this section's Rest meditation song as you take time to seek God in secret spaces.

SEEKING GOD

Soul, you must seek yourself in Me
And in yourself seek Me.

With such skill, soul,
Love could portray you in Me
That a painter well gifted
Could never show
So finely that image.

For love you were fashioned
Deep within me
Painted so beautiful, so fair;
If, my beloved, I should lose you,
Soul, in yourself seek Me.

Well I know that you will
discover
Yourself portrayed in my heart
So lifelike drawn
It will be a delight to behold
Yourself so well painted.

And should by chance you do
not know
Where to find Me,
Do not go here and there;
But if you wish to find Me,
In yourself seek Me.

Soul, since you are My room,
My house and dwelling,
If at any time,
Through your distracted ways
I find the door tightly closed.

Outside yourself seek Me not,
To find Me it will be
Enough only to call Me,
Then quickly will I come,
And in yourself seek Me.

— St. Teresa of Ávila[12]

Image: The Cathedral of the Savior in Ávila, Spain

SECTION 2

Holy Father

Pray then in this way: Our Father in heaven, hallowed be your name." (Mt 6:9)

Image: The view of the Sea of Galilee near the Mount of the Beatitudes, Israel

DEEP DIVE INTO SCRIPTURE: MATTHEW 6:9

To study this verse in context, we will first explore other verses in Scripture that also use the words Father and holy. Since the New Testament was written in Greek, we've included parallel verses that use the same Greek words for "father" (*patēr*) and "holy" (*hagiazō*). Look up and write out the verses below using your own Bible translation. Engaging in this exercise helps us understand the passage in the full context of Scripture and can show how these verses apply to yesterday, today, and forever.

Word/Phrase	Verse	Write Out His Word
father (English) *patēr* (Greek)	Isaiah 63:16	
	Isaiah 64:8[1]	
	1 John 3:1	
holy, set apart (English) *hagiazō* (Greek)	Ezekiel 36:23	
	Hebrews 2:11–12	
	1 Peter 1:15–16	

IN THE FAMILY

The doctrine of "sonship" and the personal nature of calling God our own Father is unique to Christianity. As Christians, we say this confidently because through baptism we are adopted into the family of God as children of God. This is the instruction from Christ himself.

This is also why Jesus taught the prayer to his disciples in this way, as one calling upon the Father as a child does. Jesus could have prayed "Our Lord," or "Our King," but he intentionally used "Our Father," two words that teach us a great lesson while presenting a great challenge. As theologian Timothy Keller once said, "The only person who dares wake up a king at 3:00 a.m. for a glass of water is a child. We have that kind of access."

The Greek word for "father" that is used in the New Testament is *patēr*, which means a literal (not figurative) father.[2] The word intentionally suggests someone close in a relationship, like the Aramaic word Jesus used elsewhere, Abba, which could be translated "Daddy" (Mk 14:36). Beginning prayer in this way should change everything about the way we pray. For by praying "Father," we are, before all else, making a bold and confident declaration.

***patēr* (Greek) — father**

In the Old Testament, it was rare to describe God as a father in a personal way. If the term was used, it was referencing God as the father of the people of Israel. Sometimes a prophet used the word when he prayed. For instance, the prophet Isaiah wrote, "For you are our father (*patēr*), though Abraham does not know us and Israel does not acknowledge us; you, O LORD, are our father; our Redeemer from of old is your name" (Is 63:16).

In the psalms, King David uses a simile to compare God's love with a father's compassion for his children: "As a father (*patēr*) has compassion for his children, so the LORD has compassion for those who fear him" (Ps 103:13).

Isaiah refers to God the Father as more of a creator: "Yet, O LORD you are our Father (*patēr*); we are the clay, and you are our potter; we are all the work of your hand" (Is 64:8).[3]

This imagery is beautiful but still distances the Israelites as mere "clay," not as sons or daughters. Jesus transforms the relationship between us and the Father, inviting us into his own relationship with God. When he teaches us how to pray, he begins by calling on God as *patēr*, not King or Lord, which further reinforces this relationship for those who believe.

As John writes: "See what love the Father (*patēr*) has given us, that we should be called children of God; and that is what we are. The reason the world does not know us is that it did not know him" (1 Jn 3:1).

Outside of this prayer, throughout the four Gospels, Jesus reiterates to his disciples that God is Father, because we gain an inheritance through Jesus the Son. "Look at the birds of the air; they neither sow nor reap nor gather into barns, and yet your heavenly Father feeds them. Are you not of more value than they?" (Mt 6:26).

Jesus teaches us that the Lord cares deeply for each of us, and that the relationship he has with the Father is possible for us as well. "Do not be afraid, little flock, for it is your Father's good pleasure to give you the kingdom" (Lk 12:32).

Jesus makes it possible for us to call upon God as our real and personal Father. It is a wonderful invitation, but calling God "Father" is also challenging. For what is the expectation of the child but to reflect the image of the parent?

TO BE SANCTIFIED

"Hallowed be thy name." The Greek word hagios or *hagiazō* is a verb that means to be made holy, to sanctify.[4] Of course, we don't sanctify or make God the Father holy when we pray this way; rather, Jesus calls us to pray this way as an invitation to us. Since our Father is holy, so should we be made holy.

hagiazō **(Greek) — to be holy, set apart**

Since we are God's children, our lives should reflect his holiness. The Prophet Ezekiel in the Old Testament quotes the Lord, saying, "I will sanctify (*hagiazō*) my great name, which has been profaned among the nations, and which you have profaned among them; and the nations shall know that I am the LORD says the Lord GOD, when through you I display my holiness (*hagiazō*) before their eyes" (Ez 36:23).

As God's children, we should be praying that his holiness will be displayed in us. In his letter to the Romans, Saint Paul writes: "For the one who sanctifies (*hagiazō*) and those who are sanctified (*hagiazō*) all have one Father. For this reason Jesus is not ashamed to call them brothers and sisters, saying, 'I will proclaim your name to my brothers and sisters, in the midst of the congregation I will praise you'" (Heb 2:11–12).

Peter echoes this in his words to the early Church: "Instead, as he who called you is holy (hagios), be holy (hagios) yourselves in all your conduct; for it is written, 'You shall be holy, for I am holy'" (1 Pt 1:15–16).

In just the first line of this prayer, "Our Father in heaven, hallowed be your name," our intentions are immediately oriented toward the foundation of our faith. We have been baptized into the family of God through Jesus.

In his letter to the Corinthians, Paul encourages:

What agreement has the temple of God with idols? For we are the temple of the living God; as God said,

"I will live in them and walk among them, and I will be their God, and they shall be my people. Therefore come out from them, and be separate from them, says the Lord, and touch nothing unclean; then I will welcome you, and I will be your father, and you shall be my sons and daughters, says the Lord Almighty." (2 Cor 6:16–18)

Before even stating our needs, we have told our Father that we believe we are his children, that we recognize his holiness, and that we desire to be made further into his likeness. By using the word "our," Jesus welcomes us to share in this relationship with his Father. It's a bold way to start a conversation with the Creator of the Universe!

Reflect

REFLECTION FROM AN EARLY CHURCH FATHER

"See how he straightway stirred up the hearer, and reminded him of all God's bounty in the beginning. For he who calls God Father, by him both remission of sins, and taking away of punishment, and righteousness, and sanctification, and redemption, and adoption, and inheritance, and brotherhood with the Only-Begotten, and the supply of the Spirit, are acknowledged in this single title. For one cannot call God Father, without having attained to all those blessings. Doubly, therefore, does he awaken their spirit, both by the dignity of him who is called on, and by the greatness of the benefits which they have enjoyed. But when he says, in Heaven, he speaks not this as shutting up God there, but as withdrawing him who is praying from earth, and fixing him in the high places, and in the dwellings above.

He teaches, moreover, to make our prayer common, in behalf of our brethren also. For he says not, my Father, which art in Heaven, but, our Father, offering up his supplications for the body in common, and nowhere looking to his own, but everywhere to his neighbor's good. And by this he at once takes away hatred, and quells pride, and casts out envy, and brings in the mother of all good things, even charity, and exterminates the inequality of human things, and shows how far the equality reaches between the king and the poor man, if at least in those things which are greatest and most indispensable, we are all of us fellows.

... He commands him who prays to seek that he may be glorified also by our life. Which very thing he had said before likewise, Let your light so shine before men, that they may see your good works, and glorify your Father which is in heaven (Matthew 5:16) ... and the seraphim too, giving glory, said on this wise, "Holy, holy, holy." So that hallowed means this ... that we may live so purely, that through us all may glorify you."

— St. John Chrysostom[5]

As you ponder these verses, journal your thoughts in the space provided. Reflect on the Scripture passage (and subsequent supporting passages) from "Read." Is there a word or phrase that especially stands out to you? What do these verses say to you? What is the Holy Spirit showing you in these Scripture passages?

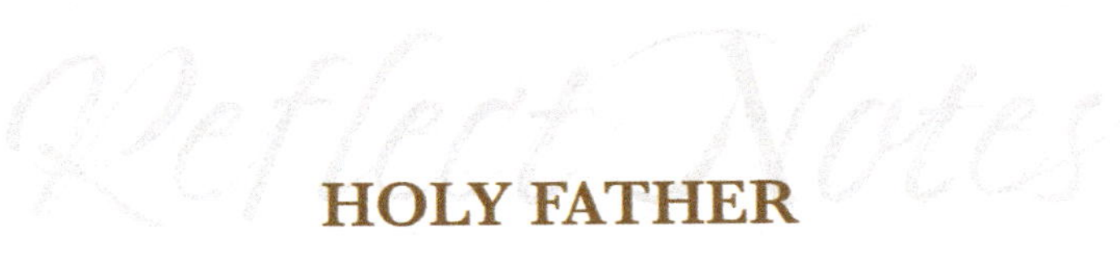

HOLY FATHER

Image: The outdoor garden of Teresa's childhood home in Ávila, Spain

Respond

In this section, we will review Teresa's response to God's word. May she serve as an example as you seek out how the Holy Spirit is prompting you to respond.

PLEASING THE FATHER

Teresa Sánchez de Cepeda y Ahumada grew up in a faithful Catholic Christian family in the stunningly fortified, walled city of Ávila, Spain. She was the sixth of twelve children, and her father and mother set a good example of Christian faith. Of her parents, she wrote: "It was a help to me to see that my parents favored nothing but virtue. And they themselves possessed many."[6]

Young Teresa had an early gift of zealous faith. At the tender age of seven, she longed to see God. Upon learning that the martyrs of the faith immediately went to heaven, she and her brother Rodrigo set off for the land of the Moors to be martyrs themselves. She wrote, "It seemed to me the price [the martyrs] paid for going to enjoy God was very cheap."[7]

Thankfully for us, the children were stopped by their uncle. As consolation, they settled on creating lovely little hermitages in their garden, planning to spend the remainder of their days as hermits.

One can't help but smile at this beautiful, innocent, devoted faith. But as happens in life, in her teenage years Teresa became caught up in worldly vanities.

Teresa and her mother would share in the love of books on chivalry, the same way mothers and daughters today share favorite books, shows, or movies. Whereas this didn't affect her mother's duties or her focus on virtue, it chipped away at Teresa's. She tried desperately to hide it well, as she always wanted to preserve her reputation. But at that time, her desire was not to preserve her honor for the secret eyes of the Lord but for the outward approval of others.

When her mother passed away, Teresa turned to these books to escape. Her vice led to new challenges as, with the absence of her mother, Teresa spent more time with her cousins. According to Teresa, they were people "who do not know the vanity of the world but rather are just getting ready to throw themselves into it." Young Teresa was swept up alongside them.

Whereas Teresa's parents had drawn her close to God, her cousins began to drag her away. One of these relationships was so bad that it convinced her father to send Teresa to a boarding school in an Augustinian convent.

Reflecting on this time in her life, Teresa later saw how her desire to please her father and others by appearing to be virtuous was misplaced. She needed, instead, to please and delight her Heavenly Father. She writes: "O my God! What harm is done in the world by considering our actions of only little importance and by thinking something can be done against you in secret! I am certain that great evils would be avoided if we were to understand that the whole matter lies not in our guarding ourselves against men but in our guarding ourselves against displeasing you."[8]

Boarding school served Teresa well. She felt her soul return to the good habits of her childhood. Then, an illness pulled her out of school and landed her in the care of her uncle, and this is where her faith began to truly deepen. The uncle asked Teresa to read to him, which exposed her to religious books that she otherwise might never have read. The result was the emergence of a desire to live the rest of her life as a nun.

Her love of chivalrous stories and romances transformed into a love for religious books. And it was through such a book, the *Letters of St. Jerome*, that she found the courage to tell her father of her longing to fully join with Jesus as a religious sister.

Her father, however, wasn't eager for her to enter a convent. He agreed that she could follow her vocation, but only after he had died. Teresa decided she could not wait that long, so she did something in disobedience to her earthly father but in obedience to her heavenly one. At age twenty, along with her brother Antonio, who also desired religious life, she stole away in the early morning.

Teresa fled to the Monastery of the Incarnation, a Carmelite order of nuns just outside the walls of the city. As much as she was happy to go, leaving her father was devastating. She writes:

> I remember, clearly and truly, that when I left my father's house I felt that separation so keenly that the feeling will not be greater, I think, when I die. For it seemed that every bone in my body was being sundered. Since there was no love of God to take away my love for my father and relatives, everything so constrained me that if the Lord hadn't helped me, my reflections would not have been enough for me to continue on. In this situation he gave me such courage against myself that I carried out the task.[9]

This suffering was rewarded. As soon as she took the habit, she was granted a happiness that never left her. She adds, "The Lord gave me an understanding of how he favors those who use force with themselves to serve him."[10]

With her lovable personality, Teresa was welcomed at the convent, where she grew in popularity. Her father eventually accepted her decision and donated a large sum to the convent, as was the custom at the time.

Although she was happy, it would be twenty years until Teresa would experience the mystical relationship with God we think of when we think of her today. Everything up until this point was simple obedience to God, as she recognized herself as a daughter of the heavenly Father — truly a first step. This decision was the beginning of her detachment, although she was unaware what detachment was, or even all she still had left to surrender.

Near the end of her life, after her profound mystical experiences, Teresa expanded on her love of God as Father in her book *The Way of Perfection*. Most of her commentary on this first part of the Lord's Prayer, written for her religious sisters, focuses on the phrase "who art in heaven," and how we can turn inward and soar to heaven within ourselves to find the King of Kings.

> Oh, daughters, how readily should perfect contemplation come at this point! Oh, how right it would be for the soul to enter within itself in order to rise the better above itself that this holy Son might make it understand the nature of the place where he says his Father dwells, which is in the heavens. Let us go forth from the earth, my daughters, for there is no reason that a favor like this should be so little esteemed, that after we have understood how great it is, we should still want to remain on earth.[11]

To Teresa, our soul is the castle where the King dwells. The fact that the King would even desire to dwell within us emboldens her imagination:

> Well, let us imagine that within us is an extremely rich palace, built entirely of gold

> and precious stones; in sum, built for a lord such as this. Imagine, too, as is indeed so, that you have a part to play in order for the palace to be so beautiful, for there is no edifice as beautiful as is a soul pure and full of virtues. The greater the virtues, the more resplendent the jewels. Imagine, also, that in this palace dwells this mighty King who has been gracious enough to become your Father; and that he is seated upon an extremely valuable throne, which is your heart.[12]

Teresa's sisters-in-religion were more comfortable with vocal prayer than mental prayer. So, Teresa turned to the prayer prayed most often with vocal prayer, the Our Father, to teach them to pray more deeply. She challenged her fellow nuns to use vocal prayer as a means to enter mental prayer and, hopefully, contemplative prayer. "What I would like us to do daughters, is refuse to be satisfied with merely pronouncing the words, For when I say, 'I believe,' it seems to me right that I should know and understand what I believe. And when I say, 'Our Father,' it will be an act of love to understand who this Father of ours is and who the Master is who taught us this prayer."[13]

Teresa recognized that the Our Father unites us with the teacher of the prayer, Jesus. And when we pray it, these words, this time with Our Lord, are meant to transform us: "Does it seem right to you now that even though we recite these first words vocally we should fail to let our intellects understand and our hearts break in pieces at seeing such love? What son is there in the world who doesn't strive to learn who his father is when he knows he has such a good one with so much majesty and power?"[14]

Teresa, who had such a good earthly father, found an even greater one in heaven. In this supernatural relationship, she would eventually find intimate friendship. Remarkably, we see this didn't happen with just her single act of choosing religious life. She herself needed that first step of obedience, that first step of detachment from a world of distractions. From there, God could lead her into a deeper relationship than she could have imagined. But that beginning brought her to the place where the Father could whisper to his beloved daughter.

DISCUSSION QUESTIONS

1.How did Teresa grow up and how did she change in her early teenage years?

2. What were some of the moments that led her to religious life?

3. How does Teresa's view of the Our Father make the prayer more intimate?

4. Have you ever thought of your soul as a place where God dwells? How does this knowledge change the way you pray?

5. Do you see God as a Father? How does this change the way you approach him?

6. What holds you back from a quiet prayer life?

You shall be holy, for I am holy.

(1 PT 1:16)

Image: The Cathedral of the Savior in Ávila, Spain

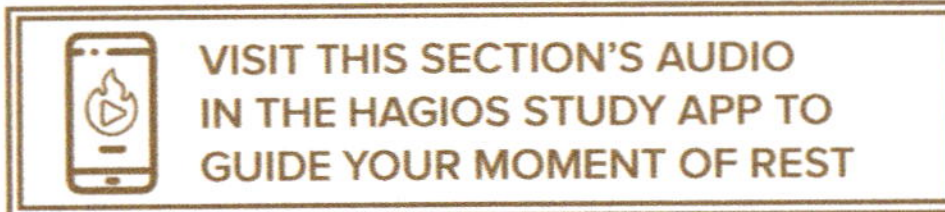

Below is a poem from St. Teresa of Ávila on surrendering one's life completely to the will of God the Father. We encourage you to use it during your time of prayer. As you finish this part of the study, visit the Hagios Study mobile app for this section's Rest meditation song as you take some time to be with the Father.

IN THE HANDS OF GOD

I am Yours and born of You,
What do You want of me?

Majestic Sovereign,
Unending wisdom,
Kindness pleasing to my soul;
God sublime, one Being Good,
Behold this one so vile.
Singing of her love to you:
What do You want of me?

Yours, you made me,
Yours, you saved me,
Yours, you endured me,
Yours, you called me,
Yours, you awaited me,
Yours, I did not stray.
What do You want of me? …

Give me, if You will, prayer;
Or let me know dryness,
And abundance of devotion,
Or if not, then barrenness.
In you alone, Sovereign Majesty,
I find my peace,
What do You want of me? …

Silent or speaking,
Fruitbearing or barren,
My wounds shown by the Law,
Rejoicing in the tender Gospel;
Sorrowing or exulting,
You alone live in me:
What do You want of me?

Yours I am, for You I was born:
What do You want of me?

— St. Teresa of Ávila[15]

Image: The exterior medieval walls of Ávila, Spain

SECTION 3

Kingdom

“

Your kingdom come. Your will be done, on earth as it is in heaven.” (Mt 6:10)

Image: A panoramic view of Jerusalem from the Mount of Olives, Israel

DEEP DIVE INTO SCRIPTURE: MATTHEW 6:10

To study this verse in context, we will first explore other verses in Scripture that also use the words kingdom and will. Since the New Testament was written in Greek, we've included parallel verses that use the same Greek word for kingdom (*basileia*) or will (*thelēma*). Look up and write out these verses below using your own Bible translation. Engaging in this exercise helps us understand the passage in the full context of Scripture and can show how these verses apply to yesterday, today, and forever.

Word/Phrase	Verse	Write Out His Word
kingdom (English) *basileia* (Greek)	Daniel 2:44	
	Luke 12:31–34	
	Luke 17:20–21	
will, desire (English) *thelēma* (Greek)	Psalm 40:6–8	
	Matthew 7:21	
	Romans 12:2	

SEEKING HIS KINGDOM

After acknowledging God as our Father and the holiness we seek to reflect, we arrive at another characteristic of our sonship: participation in the will of our Father. As children of God, we want what the Father wants, for his way is perfect. This was the central message of Jesus during his ministry on earth; he wanted us to understand and then desire God's will and his kingdom.

basileia (Greek) — kingdom

The word for kingdom in Greek is *basileia*, which is widespread throughout both the Old and New Testaments.[1] After the loss of their early kingdom, Israel began to receive prophecies of an everlasting kingdom. God was revealing to them the plan he had always had for them, set into motion after the Fall in the Garden of Eden.

The Prophet Daniel foretold: "And in the days of those kings the God of heaven will set up a kingdom (*basileia*) that shall never be destroyed, nor shall this kingdom be left to another people. It shall crush all these kingdoms and bring them to an end, and it shall stand forever" (Dn 2:44).

Later, he adds, "The kingship and dominion and the greatness of the kingdoms under the whole heaven shall be given to the people of the holy ones of the Most High; their kingdom (*basileia*) shall be an everlasting kingdom, and all dominions shall serve and obey them" (Dn 7:27).

King David acknowledges that God's kingdom reigns in heaven and on earth as he proclaims: "Your kingdom is an everlasting kingdom, and your dominion endures throughout all generations. The LORD is faithful in all his words, and gracious in all his deeds" (Ps 145:13).

The Israelites believed the Messiah would establish a kingdom forever in the earthly sense, conquering earthly empires and providing abundant earthly riches. It took Jesus' entire earthly ministry of three years to set the record straight. Instead of earthly power and wealth, Jesus teaches: "Instead, strive for his kingdom (*basileia*), and these things will be given to you as well. Do not be afraid, little flock, for it is your Father's good pleasure to give you the kingdom. Sell your possessions, and give alms. Make purses for yourselves that do not wear out, an unfailing treasure in heaven, where no thief comes near and no moth destroys. For where your treasure is, there your heart will be also" (Lk 12:31–34).

Of the forty-three parables Jesus told, thirteen were about explaining the kingdom of God. Jesus brings the kingdom to us so we may serve others as he did, as we read in Luke's Gospel: "Once Jesus was asked by the Pharisees when the kingdom of God was coming, and he answered, 'The kingdom (*basileia*) of God is not coming with things that can be observed; nor will they say, 'Look, here it is!' or 'There it is!' For, in fact, the kingdom of God is among you" (Lk 17:20–21).

As children of the Father, what are our responsibilities with this kingdom? It has everything to do with acknowledging that the Father is King and embracing his perfect will.

WHAT GOD DESIRES

The Greek word for will is *thelēma*, a noun that means "will," "desire," or "pleasure."[2] Considering this verse through the lens of "desire" can help us make it more applicable to our lives, as it's a word we recognize a bit more readily. So we might pray, "Your kingdom come, your desire be done."

thelēma (Greek) — will, desire, pleasure

Before we even bring our "wants" to God, we

ask first for his desires, his will, to be done.

The psalmist David sings: "Sacrifice and offering you do not desire, but you have given me an open ear. Burnt offering and sin offering you have not required. Then I said, 'Here I am; in the scroll of the book it is written of me. I delight to do your will (*thelēma*), O my God; your law is within my heart'" (Ps 40:6–8).

Who else is there to delight to do the will of the Father but the children of the Father? David's psalms are a great reminder that we aren't born simply knowing God's desires; rather, they are taught to us. Through our free will, we can live them out.

Thus the psalmist prays, "Teach me to do your will [*thelēma*], for you are my God. Let your good spirit lead me on a level path" (Ps 143:10).

Paul echoes this in the New Testament: "Do not be conformed to this world, but be transformed by the renewing of your minds, so that you may discern what is the will [*thelēma*] of God — what is good and acceptable and perfect" (Rom 12:2).

In these verses, we pray not only that God's kingdom "come" and that what he desires be done here on earth, but that we will join with him in this kingdom eternally — the kingdom after our earthly death. Jesus boldly states, "Not everyone who says to me, 'Lord, Lord,' will enter the kingdom (*basileia*) of heaven, but only the one who does the will (*thelēma*) of my Father in heaven" (Mt 7:21).

Again, Jesus' words in the Our Father point to a prayer for disciples, a prayer for children who recognize their sonship, a sonship that Jesus invites us into as he reminds us, "For whoever does the will (*thelēma*) of my Father in heaven is my brother and sister and mother" (Mt 12:50).

Doing as God asks isn't easy. Jesus knows the challenge of participating with God in his will. This was never more true than in the Garden of Gethsemane before Jesus' crucifixion. He knew the Father's pleasing and perfect desire was the Son's total sacrifice: "For I have come down from heaven, not to do my own will (*thelēma*), but the will of him who sent me" (Jn 6:38).

The words we pray are simple: "Your kingdom come, your will be done." Yet it's important to consider the depth of that request. These are not simple words of praise that we utter as slaves or peasant subjects of the King. As we see throughout the Old and New Testaments, for us as sons and daughters of the King, these words are an invitation to an inheritance.

Reflect

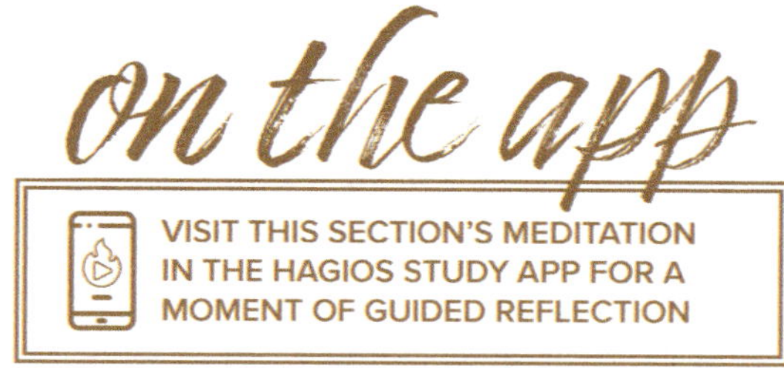

REFLECTION FROM EARLY CHURCH FATHERS

"Moreover, we ask that the will of God may be done both in heaven and in earth, each of which things pertains to the fulfillment of our safety and salvation. For since we possess the body from the earth and the spirit from heaven, we ourselves are earth and heaven; and in both — that is, both in body and spirit — we pray that God's will may be done. For between the flesh and spirit there is a struggle; and there is a daily strife as they disagree one with the other, so that we cannot do those very things that we would, in that the spirit seeks heavenly and divine things, while the flesh lusts after earthly and temporal things; and therefore we ask that, by the help and assistance of God, agreement may be made between these two natures, so that while the will of God is done both in the spirit and in the flesh, the soul which is new-born by him may be preserved."

— Cyprian of Carthage, *Treatise 4: On the Lord's Prayer;* AD 250–258[3]

"Your kingdom come" is not used in such a way as if God were not now reigning. But some one perhaps might say the expression "come" meant "upon earth"; as if, indeed, he were not even now really reigning upon earth, and had not always reigned upon it from the foundation of the world. Come, therefore, is to be understood in the sense of manifested to men. For in the same way also as a light which is present is absent to the blind, and to those who shut their eyes; so the kingdom of God, though it never departs from the earth, is yet absent to those who are ignorant of it.

And therefore, after that petition where we say, "Your kingdom come," there follows, "Your will be done, as in heaven so in earth": i.e., just as your will is in the angels who are in heaven, so that they wholly cleave to you, and thoroughly enjoy you, no error beclouding their wisdom, no misery hindering their blessedness; so let it be done in your saints who are on earth, and made from the earth, so far as the body is concerned, and who, although it is into a heavenly habitation and exchange, are yet to be taken from the earth. "

— St. Augustine of Hippo[4]

As you ponder these verses, journal your thoughts in the space provided. Reflect on the Scripture passage (and subsequent supporting passages) from "Read." Is there a word or phrase that especially stands out to you? What do these verses say to you? What is the Holy Spirit showing you in these Scripture passages?

KINGDOM

Image: Monastery of the Incarnation in Ávila, Spain

Respond

In this section, we will review Teresa's response to God's word. May she serve as an example as you seek out how the Holy Spirit is prompting you to respond.

ATTACHED TO HER WILL

The same desire Teresa had when she was seven, to run away and "see God," resurfaced and reignited as she entered the Monastery of the Incarnation. However, encountering God wouldn't come quickly or easily.

Located on the outskirts of the famous Ávila walls, the convent did not practice enclosure, so outsiders were free to visit, to come and go as they pleased. Teresa's vibrant and likable personality attracted friends quickly both inside and outside the religious house. Many days were spent in conversation in the convent parlor, building relationships and enjoying the company of others.

Many noble people sought out a relationship with Teresa; the same was true for her confessors. Teresa was, for lack of a better term, "popular." In her later years, Teresa reflected on this time with tremendous sadness, describing it as a time of many sins. She recognized this vanity, or desire to be liked, as a desire to not feel any kind of scorn. In seeking approval from others she found herself slipping into untruths and pretenses: "I enjoyed being esteemed. I was meticulous about everything I did. It all seemed to me virtue, although this will be no reason for pardon, because I knew in everything what seeking my own happiness was, and thus ignorance is no excuse."[5]

Soon after entering religious life, Teresa got very ill and nearly died. In fact, at one point she was so ill the convent thought her dead and was preparing to return her body to her family for burial. To their surprise, Teresa was very much alive, though the effects of her illness left her paralyzed for eight months, with additional bodily effects that went on for years.

Suffering in this way brought Teresa further from her own desires and closer to the Lord's will:

> It greatly profited me to have read the story of Job. … For it seems the Lord prepared me by this means, together with my having begun to experience prayer, so that I could be able to bear the suffering with so much conformity to his will. All my conversations were with him. I kept these words of Job very habitually in my mind and recited them: Since we receive good things from the hand of the Lord, why do we not suffer the evil things? This it seems gave me strength.[6]

Teresa began to rely on prayer to help her through suffering. She felt a pull to ask for the intercession of Saint Joseph, the earthly father of Jesus. She attributed much of her miraculous healing to Saint Joseph's intercession as she became conformed to the will of God.

Once fully recovered, however, the saint slipped back into a lapse of prayer under the guise of humility, saying she was too sinful to approach God in prayer:

> Since I thus began to go from pastime to pastime, from vanity to vanity, from one occasion to another, to place myself so often in very serious occasions, and to allow my

> soul to become so spoiled by many vanities, I was then ashamed to return to the search for God by means of a friendship as special as is that found in the intimate exchange of prayer.
>
> And I was aided in this vanity by the fact that as the sins increased I began to lose joy in virtuous things and my taste for them. … It seemed to me that, since in being wicked I was among the worst, it was better to go the way of the many, to recite what I was obliged to vocally and not to practice mental prayer and so much intimacy with God, for I merited to be with the devils. And it seemed to me that I was deceiving people since exteriorly I kept up such good appearances. Thus the convent where I resided was not at fault. For in my craftiness I strove to be held in esteem.[7]

This wandering away from prayer was made most apparent to Teresa when her father died. He had always been a virtuous man, but during her illness and recovery, Teresa had shared with him the benefits of her active prayer life, all before a false humility had deceived her into abandoning talking with God in mental prayer. Teresa recalls that by the time her father passed away, his devoted and deep prayer life made her ashamed of the emptiness of her own.

Outwardly, Teresa seemed the same to others. They knew nothing of her lack of prayer or the vanities that contributed to her sins. During this time, her confessors were of no help. Either they misled Teresa into thinking that her seeking the approval of others and an exterior appearance of virtue were not sins, or they thought so highly of her outward expression of faith that they never challenged or questioned her spiritual state.

It wasn't until a fateful experience in front of a statue of a scourged Christ before Pontius Pilate (the *ecce homo,* or "Behold the man") that God awakened her heart to turn from a false humility toward true humility and to seek him in prayer. Teresa describes this as the only way to truly know the will of the Lord:

> For mental prayer in my opinion is nothing else than an intimate sharing between friends, it means taking time frequently to be alone with him who we know loves us. In order that love be true and the friendship endure, the wills of the friends must be in accord. The will of the Lord, it is already known, cannot be at fault; our will is vicious, sensual, and ungrateful. And if you do not yet love him as he loves you because you have not reached the degree of conformity with his will, you will endure this pain of spending a long while with one who is so different from you when you see how much it benefits you to possess his friendship and how much he loves you.[8]

Her experience before the image of Christ and her reading of Augustine's *Confessions* brought change to Teresa's private prayer life. God was at work within her as she gave herself over to alone time with him in mental prayer. Out of this surrender of her will to his, beautiful fruit began to form. Soon to follow were the mystical encounters and spiritual favors we have come to know when we think of Teresa.

After years of intimacy and favor with God, Teresa wrote extensively about the benefits of detaching our will to accept his will. In her own detachment, Teresa found the kingdom of God, and she desired that everyone do the same. In *The Way of Perfection*, Teresa reflects on the passage "May your will be done, on earth as it is in heaven":

> Now behold, daughters, how great the wisdom of our Master is. I am reflecting here on what we are asking for when we ask for this kingdom, and it is good that we understand our request. But since his

> Majesty saw that we could neither hallow, nor praise, nor extol, nor glorify this holy name of the Eternal Father in a fitting way, because of the tiny amount we ourselves are capable of doing, he provided for us by giving us here on earth his kingdom.[9]

Teresa encouraged her sisters to abandon all fear in detaching from their own will. She knew all too well the negative effect of caring about what others may think, or of distancing oneself from God through false humility. Instead, true humility is knowing the Lord is God of all, and his perfect will never means destitution or abandonment. "But certainly, my Lord, you do not leave us empty-handed when we give you everything we can — I mean if we really give it, as we say we will. Your will be done on earth as it is in heaven."[10]

She encourages her sisters:

> How our will deviates in its inclination from that which is the will of God. He wants us to love truth; we love the lie. He wants us to desire the eternal; we, here below, lean toward what comes to an end. He wants us to desire sublime and great things; we, here below, desire base and earthly things. He would want us to desire only what is secure; we, here below, love the dubious. Everything is a mockery, my daughters, except beseeching God to free us from these dangers forever and draw us at last away from every evil. Even though our desire may not be perfect, let us force ourselves to make the request. What does it cost us to ask for a great deal? We are asking it of One who is powerful. But in order to be right, let us leave the giving to his will since we have already given him our own. His name be forever hallowed in heaven and on earth, and may his will be always done in me. Amen.[11]

For Teresa detachment from her own will began when she humbly sought God in prayer, triggered by the *ecce homo*. In prayer, through the discipline of detachment, God could reveal his will for her life.

There is a beautiful poem often attributed to Teresa, and although it does not appear in any of her works, it undoubtedly reflects the spirit of much of her writing:

Christ has no body but yours,
No hands, no feet on earth but yours,
Yours are the eyes with which he looks
Compassion on this world,
Yours are the feet with which he walks to do
good,
Yours are the hands, with which he blesses all
the world.
Yours are the hands, yours are the feet,
Yours are the eyes, you are his body.
Christ has no body now but yours,
No hands, no feet on earth but yours,
Yours are the eyes with which he looks
compassion on this world.
Christ has no body now on earth but yours.

DISCUSSION QUESTIONS

1. What were Teresa's days like in the Monastery of the Incarnation before she learned mental prayer?

2. Do you think Teresa was correct in viewing herself as sinful during this time? Why or why not?

3. What happened to Teresa that first drew her to prayer, and what drew her back again?

4. Are there any distractions in your life that may be keeping you from time with God?

5. Was there any time of illness or grief that brought you into a deeper prayer life?

6. How is God calling you to further conform to his will in this season of your life?

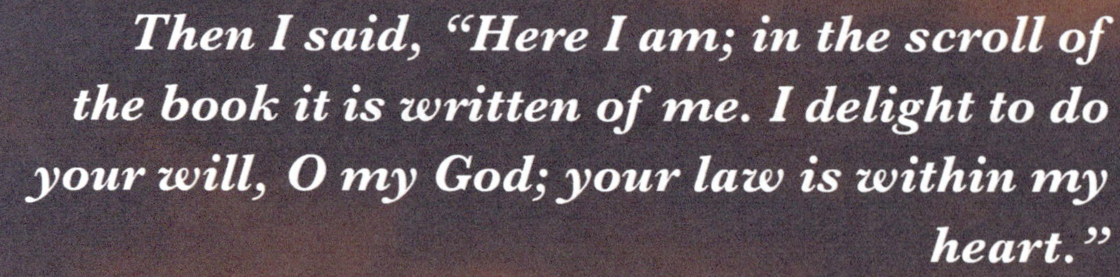

Then I said, "Here I am; in the scroll of the book it is written of me. I delight to do your will, O my God; your law is within my heart."

(PS 40:7–8)

Image: The exterior medieval walls of Ávila, Spain

Rest

VISIT THIS SECTION'S AUDIO IN THE HAGIOS STUDY APP TO GUIDE YOUR MOMENT OF REST

Below is an excerpt from Teresa's *The Way of Perfection* on surrendering her will to the Father. Use this prayer during your quiet time of rest with God today. As you finish this part of the study, visit the Hagios Study mobile app for this section's Rest meditation song for another means of reflecting on God's will.

FIAT VOLUNTAS TUA (THY WILL BE DONE)

Your will, Lord, be done in me in every way and manner that You, my Lord, want.

If You want it to be done with trials, strengthen me and let them come;

if with persecutions, illnesses, dishonors, and a lack of life's necessities, here I am;

I will not turn away, my Father, nor is it right that I turn my back on You.

Since Your Son gave You this will of mine in the name of all, there's no reason for any lack on my part.

But grant me the favor of Your kingdom that I may do Your will, since He asked for this kingdom for me, and use me as You would Your own possession, in conformity with Your will.

Amen.

— Teresa of Ávila[12]

Image: A sunset over the Sinai desert in Egypt

SECTION 4

Bread

“

Give us this day our daily bread.” (Mt 6:11)

Image: A desert in Egypt on the route the Israelites traveled in Exodus

DEEP DIVE INTO SCRIPTURE: MATTHEW 6:11

To study this verse in context, we will first explore other verses in Scripture that also use the word bread. Since the New Testament was written in Greek, we've included parallel verses that use the same Greek word for bread (*artos*). Look up and write out these verses below using your own Bible translation. Engaging in this exercise helps us understand the passage in the full context of Scripture and can show how these verses apply to yesterday, today, and forever.

Word/Phrase	Verse	Write Out His Word
bread (English), *artos* (Greek)	Genesis 3:19	
	Exodus 16:4	
	John 6:33–35	
	Matthew 4:4	
	Matthew 7:9–11	

THE BREAD THAT SATISFIES

Before we dig into Matthew 6:11 and the scriptural view of bread, we need to highlight something in this verse that is absolutely unique. Although our corresponding verses will study the Greek word used for bread, we cannot do a similar verse study for the Greek word translated as "daily." There are no other verses aside from the Our Father in the Gospels of Matthew and Luke that include this word: *epiousios*. The word breaks down to *epi*, meaning "above or super," and *ousia*, meaning "being."[1] We're praying for a "super being" or supernatural bread. Keep this in mind as we move forward with our verse study.

***artos* (Greek) — bread**

The Greek word *artos* simply means bread.[2] At the very beginning of Genesis, God states: "By the sweat of your face you shall eat bread (*artos*) until you return to the ground, for out of it you were taken; you are dust, and to dust you shall return" (Gn 3:19).

Bread is life, sustenance, a visual representation of our daily needs on earth until our death. Even while the Israelites wandered in the desert, God sustained and supplied them with what they needed. He did this by giving them bread from heaven: "Then the Lord said to Moses, 'I am going to rain bread (*artos*) from heaven for you, and each day the people shall go out and gather enough for that day. In that way I will test them, whether they will follow my instruction or not'" (Ex 16:4).

Every day the Lord gave them just enough manna for one day. When the Israelites disobediently tried to save it, it would spoil. "And Moses said to them, 'Let no one leave any of it over until morning.' But they did not listen to Moses; some left part of it until morning, and it bred worms and became foul. And Moses was angry with them. Morning by morning they gathered it, as much as each needed; but when the sun grew hot, it melted" (Ex 16:19–21).

The manna, a supernatural gift to the Israelites, truly became their "daily bread."

When we ask God to give us our "daily bread," we remember his faithfulness in providing for our physical needs. Later in the Old Testament, the Prophet Elijah receives *artos* from God. In this instance, God uses ravens to bring him food: "The ravens brought him bread (*artos*) and meat in the morning, and bread and meat in the evening; and he drank from the wadi" (1 Kgs 17:6).

Just as God supernaturally sustained his people throughout the Old Testament, he provides for us, his children, now. He wants to give us good gifts and to sustain us. In the psalms, David sings of God, who promises, "I will abundantly bless its provisions; I will satisfy its poor with bread" (Ps 132:15).

In the New Testament, Jesus points to himself as the new, supernatural, "supersubstantial" bread: "'For the bread (*artos*) of God is that which comes down from heaven and gives life to the world.' They said to him, 'Sir, give us this bread always.' Jesus said to them, 'I am the bread of life. Whoever comes to me will never be hungry, and whoever believes in me will never be thirsty'" (Jn 6:33–35).

Jesus boldly states that he is the new manna from heaven. For Catholic Christians, this is lived out in the Eucharist. Jesus gives us the new manna (himself, in the Eucharist) while we are in the desert of exile (life on earth), journeying to the promised land (heaven).

Jesus reminds us, "[God] humbled you by letting you hunger, then by feeding you with manna, with which neither you nor your ancestors were acquainted, in order to make you understand that one does not live by bread (*artos*) alone, but by every word that comes from the mouth of the LORD" (Dt 8:3; see Mt 4:4).

In Jesus, we have the Word of God made flesh. In the Eucharist, we find the supernatural, "supersubstantial" bread. Because of this, we can seek him daily here in this life.

In many ways, when we pray to receive our "daily bread," we pray both for Jesus as the supernatural, supersubstantial bread that we consume (the One that fills our hearts), and for the fulfillment of our personal needs. Scripture encourages us to petition Our Lord daily, and to turn, ask, and seek for whatever we lack. We can find comfort in knowing God knows what we need or desire before we ask, and he delights to give to us, his children, with love.

"Is there anyone among you who, if your child asks for bread (*artos*), will give a stone? Or if the child asks for a fish, will give a snake? If you then, who are evil, know how to give good gifts to your children, how much more will your Father in heaven give good things to those who ask him!" (Mt 7:9–11).

The one who gives us the Our Father prayer is himself the "Bread of Life." He prays this prayer with us to the Father. He gives himself to us as he takes the loaf of bread in Matthew 26:26 and instructs, "Take, eat; this is my body."

So we join with the disciples as we pray this verse from the prayer that Jesus taught, continually asking him to dwell in us, saying, "[Lord], give us this bread always" (Jn 6:34).

Reflect

REFLECTION FROM AN EARLY CHURCH FATHER

"Christ is the bread of life; and this bread does not belong to all men, but it is ours. And according as we say, Our Father, because he is the Father of those who understand and believe; so also we call it our bread, because Christ is the bread of those who are in union with his body. And we ask that this bread should be given to us daily, that we who are in Christ, and daily receive the Eucharist for the food of salvation, may not … be separated from Christ's body. …

But it may also be thus understood, that we who have renounced the world, and have cast away its riches and pomps in the faith of spiritual grace, should only ask for ourselves food and support, since the Lord instructs us, and says, 'Whosoever forsakes not all that he has, cannot be my disciple' (Lk 14:33).

But he who has begun to be Christ's disciple, renouncing all things according to the word of his Master, ought to ask for his daily food, and not to extend the desires of his petition to a long period, as the Lord again prescribes, and says, 'Take no thought for the morrow, for the morrow itself shall take thought for itself. Sufficient for the day is the evil thereof' (Mt 6:34). With reason, then, does Christ's disciple ask food for himself for the day, since he is prohibited from thinking of the morrow; because it becomes a contradiction and a repugnant thing for us to seek to live long in this world, since we ask that the kingdom of God should come quickly. Thus also the blessed apostle admonishes us, giving substance and strength to the steadfastness of our hope and faith: We brought nothing, says he, into this world, nor indeed can we carry anything out. Having therefore food and raiment, let us be here with content."

— Cyprian of Carthage[3]

As you ponder these verses, journal your thoughts in the space provided. Reflect on the Scripture passage (and subsequent supporting passages) from "Read." Is there a word or phrase that especially stands out to you? What do these verses say to you? What is the Holy Spirit showing you in these Scripture passages?

BREAD

Image: An alter in the Monastery of the Incarnation in Ávila, Spain

Respond

In this section, we will review Teresa's response to God's word. May she serve as an example as you seek out how the Holy Spirit is prompting you to respond.

CONVERSING WITH ANGELS

As Teresa detached from social perception and returned to God in "the prayer of quiet," her life began to change dramatically. She began to practice mental prayer — that is, silent prayer focused on images of Christ and a desire for greater intimacy with him. At the encouragement of a confessor, she increased her reception of Communion. As she did, favors from God seemed to pour forth.

One of these was what Teresa called locutions — hearing the voice of God within. This began as she prayed the Liturgy of the Hours and meditated on Psalm 119. She felt comfort at the thought of God's power as she read the verse, "You are righteous, O LORD, and your judgments are right" (Ps 119:137). This led her to reflect on the many favors God had given her, and she wondered at this generosity, especially as she perceived herself as being so sinful compared to others.

It was then that she heard God say to her, "Serve me, and don't bother about such things."[4] Initially, she was frightened of these favors and mystical experiences, like the prayer of union, where she felt physically carried away. She feared these were perhaps spiritual attacks and temptations, because she thought herself unworthy and too sinful for these blessings.

Her concerns led her to consult with many priests about these "locutions" and her physical experiences of union with Christ during prayer. She got conflicting responses. The first of her confessors told her that these things were from the Devil and they should be resisted.

In her heart, Teresa believed these were gifts from the Lord, but in obedience to her confessor, she followed his guidance to avoid these experiences, although it brought her much pain. Eventually, the Lord brought a Jesuit priest her way, one who could understand her experiences. He encouraged the nun to always turn her intentions in prayer to what would please God and instructed her to recite the *Veni Creator Spiritus* hymn, an old Georgian chant that begins, "Come, Holy Spirit." As Teresa recited these words in prayer, she experienced a new level of union she had never experienced before, a carrying of the soul out of its senses:

> While saying it, a rapture came upon me so suddenly that it almost carried me out of myself. It was something I could not doubt, because it was very obvious. It was the first time the Lord granted me this favor of rapture. I heard these words: "No longer do I want you to converse with men but with angels." This experience terrified me because the movement of the soul was powerful and these words were spoken to me deep within the spirit; so it frightened me — although on the other hand I felt great consolation when the fear that, I think, was caused by the novelty of the experience left me.[5]

These locutions and raptures began a new depth of intimacy in prayer for Teresa. After two years of these favors and mystical experiences, Teresa began to receive visions of Christ. These first began as an awareness of Jesus next to her, on the feast day of Saint Peter:

> Being in prayer on the feast day of the glorious St. Peter, I saw or, to put it better, I felt Christ beside me; I saw nothing with my bodily eyes or with my soul, but it seemed to me that Christ was at my side — I saw that it was he, in my opinion, who was speaking to me. Since I was completely unaware that there could be a vision like this one, it greatly frightened me in the beginning; I did nothing but weep. However, by speaking one word alone to assure me, the Lord left me feeling as I usually did: quiet, favored, and without any fear. It seemed to me that Jesus Christ was always present at my side; but since this wasn't an imaginative vision, I didn't see any form. Yet I felt very clearly that he was always present at my right side and that he was the witness of everything I did. At no time in which I was a little recollected, or not greatly distracted, was I able to ignore that he was present at my side.[6]

On subsequent occasions, Jesus showed Teresa his hands and then his face. Then, on the feast day of Saint Paul, he revealed his whole self to her in his risen form, like that in a painting. These were followed by many other visions of Jesus on the cross or in the Garden of Gethsemane.

It was important for Teresa to communicate that these visions were experienced inwardly — not seen with her bodily eyes. She describes this interiority as the preferred way to have a vision, believing it was better to experience these in the mind because the mystical things of God are best communicated this way, but also because the Devil can deceive the bodily eyes.

She describes the encounter like the way Christ might communicate with us in heaven:

> It seems to me that the Lord in every way wants this soul to have some knowledge of what goes on in heaven. I think that just as in heaven you understand without speaking … so it is in this vision. For God and the soul understand each other only through the desire his Majesty has that it understand him, without the use of any other means devised to manifest the love these two friends have for each other.
>
> In the vision we are dealing with there is no possibility of fashioning it ourselves, but we must look at what the Lord desires to show us, when he desires, and as he desires.[7]

Her favors from God also included intellectual, visionary insights. Like St. Catherine of Siena, another Doctor of the Church, Teresa was able to understand and comprehend things she had never read, especially since, for a significant period, Spain had banned books in the vernacular, that is, permitting Latin but not Spanish. God comforted her and assured her that he would guide her, even if she couldn't access the books she needed to read.

Understandably, these experiences were challenging for her confessors, and they often leaned toward suspicion, interpreting these moments with Jesus as evil events from the Devil meant to cause her fear and pain. Thankfully, over time, God brought to Teresa good and holy men, who eased her fear.

As she continued to be united with Jesus in prayer, she eventually learned to discern what was from the Lord, and never doubted the experiences that left her with "jewels in the hand" — consolations that improved her virtue and deepened her love of the Lord.

Once the door of mental prayer was opened and she sought this profound union with Jesus daily, Teresa experienced a deeply moving favor that left her unable to speak:

> I saw close to me toward my left side an angel in bodily form. … I saw in his hands a large golden dart and at the end of the iron tip there appeared to be a little fire. It seemed to me this angel plunged the dart several times into my heart and that it reached deep within me. When he drew it out, I thought he was carrying off with him the deepest part of me; and he left me all on fire with great love of God.[8]

For Teresa, Jesus was her everything, her complete nourishment, her "daily bread." She needed nothing else. In writing about prayer to her sisters in *The Way of Perfection*, she saw no other way to perceive "the daily bread" of the Our Father except as her beloved, writing:

> His Majesty gave us, as I have said, the manna and nourishment of his humanity that we might find him at will and not die of hunger, save through our own fault. In no matter how many ways the soul may desire to eat, it will find delight and consolation in the most Blessed Sacrament. … He is teaching us to set our wills on heavenly things and to ask that we might begin enjoying him from here below.[9]

Even given this spiritual understanding of "daily bread," Teresa also deeply understood the physical needs of everyday life, for we all have needs as long as we are here on earth.

In *The Way of Perfection* she teaches that through contemplative prayer, asking for our daily bread can also be viewed as asking heaven to come near to us in our earthly needs:

> Contemplatives and persons already very much committed to God, who no longer desire earthly things, ask for the heavenly favors that can, through God's goodness, be given on earth. Those who still live on earth, and it is good that they live in conformity with their state in life, may ask also for bread. They must be sustained and must sustain their households. Such a petition is very just and holy, and so also is their petition for other things according to their needs.[10]

Teresa often comments on how everything was given to her and not earned — they were favors from the Lord bestowed on an undeserving person. Isn't this true for all of us? We can learn from Teresa's interior life, her examples of detachment, and her experience of drawing close to Jesus in prayer through frequent Communion and in daily mental prayer.

DISCUSSION QUESTIONS

1. What favors and experiences did the Lord give Teresa?

2. Why do you think these favors were hard for her confessors to understand?

3. What did the phrase "daily bread" in the Our Father prayer mean to Teresa?

4. What does this phrase mean to you?

5. Have you ever had experiences in prayer that you couldn't easily explain to others?

6. What ways can you alter your prayer life to better seek the Lord daily?

For the bread of God is that which comes down from heaven and gives life to the world. They said to him, "Sir, give us this bread always." Jesus said to them, "I am the bread of life. Whoever comes to me will never be hungry, and whoever believes in me will never be thirsty."

(JN 6:33–35)

Image: The rolling hills of northern Spain

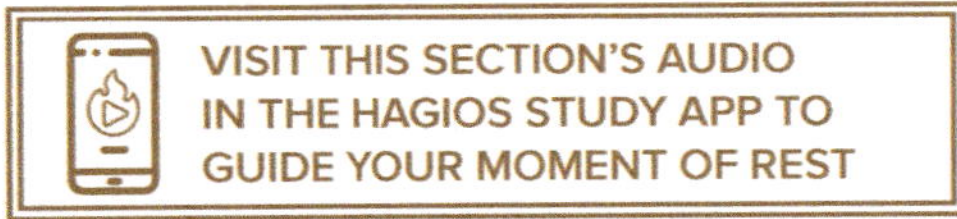

Teresa's confessor told her to direct her prayer in a way that asks God what is most pleasing to him. In doing so, he advised her to begin by reciting the hymn of St. Gregory the Great, *Veni Creator Spiritus* ("Come, Holy Spirit, Creator Blest"). Use this prayer in your time of rest. Additionally, visit the Hagios Study mobile app for this section's Rest meditation song as you continue your time in prayer.

VENI, CREATOR SPIRITUS (COME, HOLY SPIRIT, CREATOR BLEST)

Come, Holy Spirit, Creator blest,
and in our souls take up Thy rest;
come with Thy grace and heavenly aid
to fill the hearts which Thou hast made.

O comforter, to Thee we cry, O
heavenly gift of God Most High,
O fount of life and fire of love,
and sweet anointing from above.

Thou in Thy sevenfold gifts are known;
Thou, finger of God's hand we own;
Thou, promise of the Father, Thou
Who dost the tongue with power imbue.

Kindle our sense from above,
and make our hearts o'erflow with love;
with patience firm and virtue high
the weakness of our flesh supply.

Far from us drive the foe we dread,
and grant us Thy peace instead;
so shall we not, with Thee for guide,
turn from the path of life aside.

Oh, may Thy grace on us bestow
the Father and the Son to know;
and Thee, through endless times confessed,
of both the eternal Spirit blest.

Now to the Father and the Son,
Who rose from death, be glory given,
with Thou, O Holy Comforter,
henceforth by all in earth and heaven.

Amen.

Image: The shore of the Sea of Galilee, Israel

SECTION 5

Forgiven

“

And forgive us our debts, as we also have forgiven our debtors.” (Mt 6:12)

Image: A statue of St. Peter near the Primacy of St. Peter, Sea of Galilee, Israel

DEEP DIVE INTO SCRIPTURE: MATTHEW 6:12,14–15

To study these verses in context, we will first explore other verses in Scripture that also use the word forgive. Since the New Testament was written in Greek, we've included parallel verses that use the same Greek word for forgive (*aphiēmi*). Look up and write out these verses below using your own Bible translation. Engaging in this exercise helps us understand the passage in the full context of Scripture and can show how these verses apply to yesterday, today, and forever.

Word/Phrase	Verse	Write Out His Word
forgive, let go, separate (English), *aphiēmi* (Greek)	Genesis 50:17	
	Leviticus 5:10	
	Psalm 32:5	
	Matthew 18:21–22	
	Matthew 18:32–33	
	1 John 1:9	

TO LET GO

Often, we become numb to the impact of familiar words. Our brain skips over their profound meaning because we hear them too frequently or don't hear them in the proper context. Perhaps this has happened to you with the word forgive.

In Greek, the word is *aphiēmi* (af-ee'-ay-mee) and is a combination of two root words, apo, which means separation, and hiemi, which means to "send or go." In other words, it means "to let go."[1] It is also used in Scripture repeatedly to mean letting go, leaving behind, or forgiving someone their debt entirely. Earlier in our study, we learned how Teresa stated that you can enter more deeply into prayer through detachment, humility, and love of neighbor. In Matthew 6:12, we find all three.

Thinking of forgiveness as the ultimate form of detachment — a complete "letting go" — is perhaps a new perspective we can adopt when reading these supporting verses. The word *aphiēmi* is also translated in other contexts in the Bible as the phrase "to move away," "leave," and "remove."

***aphiēmi* (Greek) — leave, forgive, let go**

An early story of forgiveness in Scripture is that of Joseph (Gn 37–50), who was sold into slavery by his very own brothers. The siblings later couldn't fathom how Joseph would receive them without a grudge: "Realizing that their father was dead, Joseph's brothers said, 'What if Joseph still bears a grudge against us and pays us back in full for all the wrong that we did to him?' So they approached Joseph, saying, 'Your father gave this instruction before he died, "Say to Joseph: I beg you, forgive (*aphiēmi*) the crime of your brothers and the wrong they did in harming you." Now therefore please forgive the crime of the servants of the God of your father.' Joseph wept when they spoke to him" (Gn 50:15–17).

In the Old Testament, forgiveness came through sacrifice, as prescribed by the law: "And the second he shall offer for a burnt offering according to the regulation. Thus the priest shall make atonement on your behalf for the sin that you have committed, and you shall be forgiven (*aphiēmi*)" (Lv 5:10).

For Jesus to establish a New Covenant that involves forgiveness with reciprocity (you forgive and God will forgive you) was earth-shattering for his disciples and for the local people of the first century. Yet it is Jesus, the High Priest establishing this New Law, who creates a way for atonement. As it says in Leviticus 5:10, "Thus the priest shall make atonement on your behalf for the sin that you have committed, and you shall be forgiven (*aphiēmi*)."

As in the previous verses of the Our Father prayer, we are again sharing with Jesus. Forgiveness is possible through Jesus' sacrifice and in his role as the High Priest. Only because of him can we share in forgiving others.

The Old Testament tells the story of the Lord's faithfulness in repeatedly forgiving. His consistent forgiveness of the people of Israel is found in Exodus, Kings, and all the writings of the prophets. In the psalms, we are called back to the imagery of the secret place in which nothing is hidden from God. "Then I acknowledged my sin to you, and I did not hide my iniquity; I said, 'I will confess my transgressions to the LORD,' and you forgave (*aphiēmi*) the guilt of my sin." (Ps 32:5).

We confess, and yet the Lord always knows our sins. John the apostle writes: "If we confess our sins, he who is faithful and just will forgive (*aphiēmi*) us our sins and cleanse us from all unrighteousness" (1 Jn 1:9).

We may even try to finesse exactly what "letting

go" of a debt or transgression means, but Jesus never hides what he means. Jesus instructed Peter in this way: "Then Peter came and said to him, 'Lord, if another member of the church sins against me, how often should I forgive (*aphiēmi*)? As many as seven times?' Jesus said to him, 'Not seven times, but, I tell you, seventy-seven times'" (Mt 18:21–22).

If we truly believe in our inheritance as children of God, this part of the prayer should only encourage us that this same forgiveness is due to others, because of what we receive in abundance. We offer our forgiveness to others from a place of richness.

Jesus highlights this generosity and abundance with the parable of the unforgiving servant. In it he tells of a servant who was forgiven an enormous debt by the king but then didn't forgive a much smaller debt that was owed to him by a fellow servant. When the king learned of this, he "summoned him and said to him, 'You wicked slave! I forgave (*aphiēmi*) you all that debt because you pleaded with me. Should you not have had mercy on your fellow slave, as I had mercy on you?'" (Mt 18:32–33).

By including "forgive us our sins as we forgive others" in the prayer, Jesus teaches his disciples (and us) a powerful lesson: To forgive is to recognize our sonship with the Father.

This is so important to Our Lord that he repeats it again after the verses of the Our Father prayer, in Matthew 6:14–15. Jesus reiterates to his disciples, "For if you forgive others their trespasses, your heavenly Father will also forgive you; but if you do not forgive others, neither will your Father forgive your trespasses." Forgiveness is so important that the Lord points it out as the most essential point of the prayer!

We also find this message in the parable of the prodigal son. Jesus tells his disciples that the elder son has everything of the Father's, "All that is mine is yours" (Lk 15:31). For the elder son to forgive his brother would be to recognize there is still inheritance to be shared. We fully step into the role of sons and daughters as we call upon God the Father and forgive one another.

Our forgiveness of others impacts our relationship with the Lord. Jesus instructs, "So when you are offering your gift at the altar, if you remember that your brother or sister has something against you, leave (*aphiēmi*) your gift there before the altar and go; first be reconciled to your brother or sister, and then come and offer your gift" (Mt 5:23–24).

In forgiving our brother or sister, we "let go" of our gift at the altar in order to "let go" of another's sin against us. This also highlights the plurality of the Our Father prayer. We join in Christ, but we also join with one another in unity. In forgiveness we find the epitome of detachment, humility, and love of neighbor.

Reflect

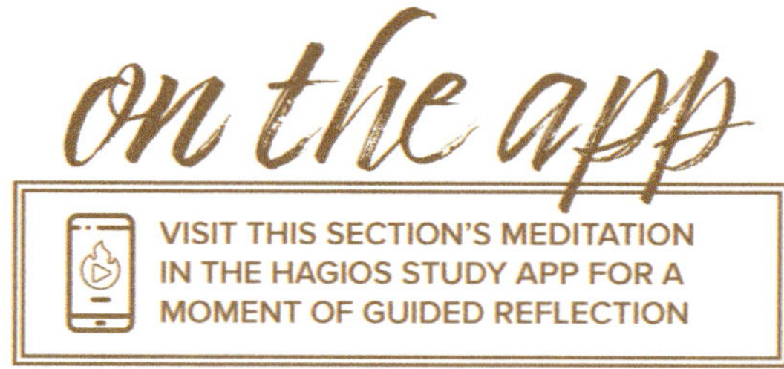

REFLECTION FROM AN EARLY CHURCH FATHER

"After the supply of food, pardon of sin is also asked for, that he who is fed by God may live in God, and that not only the present and temporal life may be provided for, but the eternal also, to which we may come if our sins are forgiven; and these the Lord calls debts, as he says in his Gospel, I forgave you all that debt, because you desired me (Matthew 18:32). And how necessarily, how providently and salutarily, are we admonished that we are sinners, since we are compelled to entreat for our sins, and while pardon is asked for from God, the soul recalls its own consciousness of sin! Lest any one should flatter himself that he is innocent, and by exalting himself should more deeply perish, he is instructed and taught that he sins daily, in that he is bidden to entreat daily for his sins. …

There remains no ground of excuse in the day of judgment, when you will be judged according to your own sentence; and whatever you have done, that you also will suffer. For God commands us to be peacemakers, and in agreement, and of one mind in his house; and such as he makes us by a second birth, such he wishes us when new-born to continue, that we who have begun to be sons of God may abide in God's peace, and that, having one spirit, we should also have one heart and one mind. …

Thus God does not receive the sacrifice of a person who is in disagreement, but commands him to go back from the altar and first be reconciled to his brother, that so God also may be appeased by the prayers of a peacemaker. Our peace and brotherly agreement is the greater sacrifice to God — and a people united in one in the unity of the Father, and of the Son, and of the Holy Spirit."

— Cyprian of Carthage[2]

As you ponder these verses, journal your thoughts in the space provided. Reflect on the Scripture passage (and subsequent supporting passages) from "Read." Is there a word or phrase that especially stands out to you? What do these verses say to you? What is the Holy Spirit showing you in these Scripture passages?

FORGIVEN

Image: The Monastery of St. Joseph in Ávila, Spain, that was founded by Teresa

Respond

In this section, we will review Teresa's response to God's word. May she serve as an example as you seek out how the Holy Spirit is prompting you to respond.

BUILDING A NEW ORDER

Teresa's new life of profound prayer impacted those around her, both for better and for worse. Some rebuked her from a place of misunderstanding and jealousy, whereas others eagerly sought to learn her spiritual practices. One of her Carmelite sisters, who embraced Teresa's revelations on prayer, felt that their prayer life would be better nurtured in a different kind of monastery. Although Teresa was very content at the Monastery of the Incarnation, she decided to take this desire to the Lord — and she was surprised by the Lord's response:

> One day after Communion, his Majesty earnestly commanded me to strive for this new monastery with all my powers, and he made great promises that it would be founded and that he would be highly served in it. He said it should be called St. Joseph and that this saint would keep watch over us at one door, and our Lady at the other, that Christ would remain with us, and that it would be a star shining with great splendor. He said that even though religious orders were mitigated one shouldn't think he was little served in them; he asked what would become of the world if it were not for religious and said that I should tell my confessor what he commanded, that he was asking him not to go against this or hinder me from doing it.[3]

Through this word from the Lord, Teresa sought to establish a stricter rule of reformed Carmelite practice to better support a life of prayer. This change, however, had to be carefully pursued. She was already suffering rebuke and persecution from those around her, and this dream for a new type of monastery would make her detractors even more enraged:

> They said I was trying to make myself out to be a saint and was inventing novelties without then even having attained to the full observance of my rule or to the level of the very good and holy nuns there were in the house. (Nor do I myself believe I will ever arrive if God in his goodness doesn't do everything himself.) They said that rather it was I who was taking away the good customs and introducing those that were not — at least that I was doing what I could to introduce them and that I was capable of causing a great deal of harm. So without any fault on their part they accused me. I don't say that only the nuns did this, but there were other persons as well. They revealed truths to me because you permitted this, Lord.[4]

Because of her detachment, humility, and love of neighbor, Teresa's soul was in a place where she could see harmful actions from others as being permitted by the Lord. Since her focus was on God, she had an interior calm, making unforgiveness impossible. Whenever anyone did anything to her or against her mission, she surrendered that action to the will of God.

Teresa understood how much she had been forgiven, so she couldn't look at others as if they didn't deserve forgiveness as well. Instead, she took the negative opinions of others as a way to serve a greater purpose — to help reinforce her humility:

> When my soul reached this stage where God granted it such a great favor, the evil in me disappeared, and the Lord gave me strength to break away from it. It didn't bother me to be amid the occasions of falling and with people who formerly what used to do me harm was helping me. All things were a means for my knowing and loving God more, for seeing what owed him, and for regretting what I had been.[5]

Teresa recounts many of these rebukes. Some nuns would make fun of her and declare she was inventing things. They would gossip that she was being deceived by the Devil. Teresa even shares how they would try to exorcize demons out of her. What seems to have hurt Teresa more, however, was that much of what her fellow religious sisters or townspeople of Ávila knew about her was a result of her private conversations with her confessors being made public. These trusted priests divulged her private information, which hurt Teresa terribly. Still, she surrendered it to the will of God:

> In this respect I am speaking as one who is suffering a bitter trial because some persons with whom I have discussed my prayer are not keeping it secret, but in consulting this one and that other, they have truly done me great harm. They have spread things that should have remained very secret — these matters are not for everybody and it seemed that I was the one who published them abroad. I believe the Lord permitted it without any fault on their part so that I might suffer. I'm not saying they spoke about what I discussed with them in confession. But since they were persons to whom because of my fears I gave an account of myself that they might enlighten me, it seemed to me they should have kept quiet. Nonetheless, I never dared to conceal anything from these persons.[6]

Teresa regularly forgave these priests, returned frequently to confession, and continued to seek their counsel. Yet even with her forgiveness, many confessors refused to hear her confession because of the gossip in town, which grieved Teresa tremendously. Difficult as it was to experience, Teresa viewed the resistance of others as something that strengthened her soul. And just as she anticipated, going public about founding the monastery did indeed increase rebuke:

> Once when I was very worried about this, the Lord asked me why I feared since only two things could happen from it; they would either criticize me or praise him. And he explained that those who believed in the experience, would praise him and that those who did not would condemn me without fault; that either outcome would be advantageous to me, and that I shouldn't be anxious.[7]

As news spread of Teresa's efforts to call back to the original intention of the Carmelite Order, to found an enclosed monastery and a place where a life of prayer could be most fruitful, the circle of persecution grew wide. The request for a new house with a new reformed order was appalling to those of Ávila, and they saw no value in it, spreading this view with "gossip, derision, [and] saying that it was foolishness":[8]

> Several of them said I should be thrown into the prison cell; others — very few defended me somewhat. I saw clearly that in many matters my opponents were right, and sometimes I gave them explanations. Yet since I couldn't mention the main factor, which was that the Lord had commanded me to do this, I didn't know how to act; so I remained silent about the other things.[9]

Her confessor told her that her desire was

against God's will. Those in charge of approving a new order or new monastery outright rejected her proposal. In fact, Teresa's efforts were becoming scandalous, and many who would never have cared one way or the other were now insisting she stop pursuing it.

However, God, ever faithful, opened opportunities for Teresa to do as he commanded. Rejection after rejection eventually led to a creative path forward. One day the idea came to Teresa for a family member to purchase a home; then the order could take over the property to establish the new monastery. With this clever solution, the Lord knocked down all obstacles in the way:

> We agreed to carry on in total secrecy, and so I got one of my sisters who lived outside this city to buy the house and fix it up, as though it were for herself, with money the Lord provided, in certain ways, for its purchase. It would take long to recount how the Lord was looking after it, for I took great care not to do anything against obedience. But I knew that if I said anything to my superiors, everything would be lost as happened the previous time, and things would even be worse. In procuring the money, acquiring the house, signing the contract for it, and fixing it up, I went through so many trials of so many kinds that now I'm amazed I was able to suffer them … [Then] on St. Bartholomew's day the habit was received by some and the Blessed Sacrament was reserved, and with all due authority and power our monastery of our most glorious father St. Joseph was founded in 1562.[10]

By God's providence, and through Teresa's detachment, humility, and love of neighbor, the mission of reforming the Carmelite Order had officially begun.

In *The Way of Perfection*, Teresa expounds on Matthew 6:12 (the verse on forgiveness) from the Our Father: "Indeed, Jesus could have put other virtues first and said: forgive us, Lord, because we do a great deal of penance or because we pray much and fast or because we have left all for you and love you very much. He didn't say forgive us because we would give up our lives for you, or, as I say, because of other possible things. But he said only, 'forgive us because we forgive.'"[11]

Nothing could have been accomplished at this time in Teresa's life had she not forgiven those who persecuted her and pursued God's command with a forgiving heart. In many ways, she didn't even need to think of forgiving; her acts of detachment naturally lent themselves to "letting go" of the way others sinned against her.

Teresa's efforts to reform the Carmelite Order would echo throughout all religious life. Her writings on prayer and the rule of life for her "Discalced" Carmelites became necessary reforms for the Catholic Church during the sixteenth century. Teresa would never have imagined this — she couldn't have imagined it. She stayed close to God's will, detaching her own, only so his kingdom would reign. Little did she know the fruits that would continually come from her simple life of prayer.

DISCUSSION QUESTIONS

1.What stood in the way of Teresa easily carrying out the command to form a new monastery?

2. What was Teresa's attitude during this time? What things didn't bother her, and what hurt her most?

3. God's will of a new order was achieved through a clever loophole, and not traditional channels. Did that surprise you? Why or why not?

4. Teresa tirelessly fought for an environment that better supported prayer. What are some ways you may be called to "fight" for a more prayerful environment in your own life?

5. What grievances or debts from people in your life do you need to "let go"?

6. Is there anything God has asked of you that seems impossible?

If we confess our sins, he who is faithful and just will forgive us our sins and cleanse us from all unrighteousness.

(1 JN 1:9)

Image: A recreation of Teresa's room in the Convent of St. Joseph, Ávila, Spain

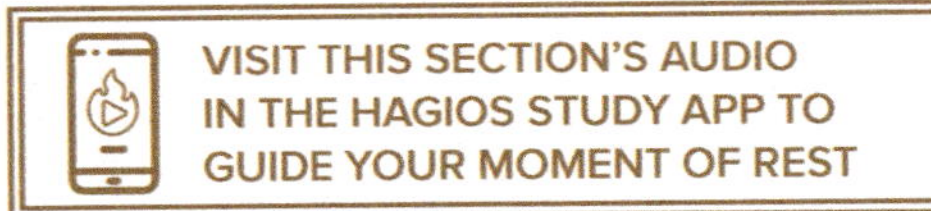

Below is a poetic prayer that was found in the margins of Teresa's breviary (a book for daily prayer) after she died. Many have called it "St. Teresa's bookmark." For us in this study, it can serve as a daily reminder that, in possessing God within us, nothing and no one should disturb us. Use this prayer for your time of rest. Additionally, as you finish this part of the study, visit the Hagios Study mobile app for this section's Rest meditation song to assist you in prayer.

LET NOTHING DISTURB YOU

Let nothing disturb you,

let nothing frighten you,

all things will pass away.

God never changes;

patience obtains all things,

whoever has God lacks nothing.

God alone suffices.

Amen.

Image: The Negev desert and Makhtesh Ramon Crater in Israel

SECTION 6
Trial

“

And do not bring us to the time of trial, but rescue us from the evil one.” (Mt 6:13)

Image: The Agony of Jesus carved into a stone in the Garden of Gethsemane

DEEP DIVE INTO SCRIPTURE: MATTHEW 6:13

To study this verse in context, look up supporting verses that also speak of "trial." Since the New Testament was written in Greek, we've included parallel verses that use the same Greek word for trial (*peirasmos*). Look up and write out these verses below using your own Bible translation. Engaging in this exercise helps us understand the passage in the full context of Scripture and can show how these verses apply to yesterday, today, and forever.

Word/Phrase	Verse	Write Out His Word
trial, temptation (English), *peirasmos* (Greek)	Exodus 17:7	
	Matthew 26:41	
	1 Corinthians 10:13	
	2 Peter 2:9	
	James 1:12	

TIME OF TRIAL

We began this study with a desire for a deeper prayer life. Through the Scripture verses and Teresa's example, I hope you have adopted the advice to withdraw into a secret place with your Lord, recognize that you are a son or daughter of the Most High, detach from your will in place of seeking God's greater one, and as you seek Jesus daily, find humility and love of neighbor as you forgive those who have hurt you. We now near the end of this study, and thus the last verse of the Our Father prayer. Here we will see the payoff for everything Jesus has taught so far: a promise to sustain us in this earthly life as we await our eternal one.

The Greek word for trial is the noun *peirasmos* (pi-ras-mos), which can also mean test or temptation.[1] Since this word is a noun and not a verb, it can help us distinguish a difference between being refined by life's trials for the sake of holiness and a time of trial that puts our faith in jeopardy. Let's turn to Scripture to understand the context of a "time of trial."

***peirasmos* (Greek) — trial, temptation**

Even though the Israelites witnessed the power of the Lord as they were rescued out of Egypt, they doubted God would provide for them in the wilderness. Their faith in the Lord was so weak that they set out to test him, even after they had received the miraculous manna in the desert (the "daily bread"). Their grumbling now was for water, which the Lord did end up giving them. The Greek translation of the word Moses used in the Old Testament is helpful for us:

"[Moses] called the place Massah (*peirasmos*) and Meribah, because the Israelites quarreled and tested the LORD, saying, 'Is the LORD among us or not?'" (Ex 17:7).

The Hebrew word *massah* and the Greek word *peirasmos* are the same; they refer to "the place of trial." In the Hebrew translation of the Old Testament, the word *massah* is repeatedly used to refer to times of trial or temptation. In context, *meribah* means "quarrel" or "contention." Seeing *massah* or *peirasmos* in the context of the exodus, we can understand that to mean a time of doubt in the Lord, a lack of faith that he will provide.

David records the Lord's words in the psalms with the Lord saying: "O that today you would listen to his voice! Do not harden your hearts, as at Meribah, as on the day at Massah (*peirasmos*) in the wilderness, when your ancestors tested me, and put me to the proof, though they had seen my work" (Ps 95:7–9).

When a time of trial is seen in light of the Israelites grumbling and testing the Lord in the wilderness, we gain a deeper understanding of the type of trial we are praying that God protects us from in Matthew 6:13 — a place in which we grow so hopeless that our faith weakens into doubt.

In the Garden of Gethsemane, Jesus knew this time of trial well. Mere hours before his crucifixion, Jesus warns the disciples, "Stay awake and pray that you may not come into the time of trial; the spirit indeed is willing, but the flesh is weak" (Mt 26:41).

Jesus knew that his arrest would thrust his disciples into a dark time. If they failed to remember his promise of a forthcoming Resurrection, there was a chance they would sink into great hopelessness and doubt their Heavenly Father. Here, Jesus insists they remain in prayer. It is believed among scholars that the prayer they prayed was the prayer that Jesus taught them, the Our Father.

In the parable of the sower, from Luke chapter 13, Jesus explains what can happen in a time of trial: "The ones on the rock are those who, when they hear the word, receive it with joy. But these have no root; they believe only for a while and in a time of testing (*peirasmos*, *massah*) fall away" (Lk 8:13).

The place of trial and testing could be seen as anything that causes us to fall away from God. Our *massah*, our *peirasmos*, is the place where we lose sight of the Father and our role as sons and daughters who have access to an abundant inheritance.

The apostle Paul knew about trial and temptation. In his letter to the Church in Corinth, he writes how God provides a way out of those times with a way to endure: "No testing has overtaken you that is not common to everyone. God is faithful, and he will not let you be tested beyond your strength, but with the testing he will also provide the way out so that you may be able to endure it" (1 Cor 10:13).

Although none of us desires a time of trial, we can have complete confidence that the Lord will deliver us from despair and give us the courage to surrender our expectations for what that looks like. As Peter writes, "Then the Lord knows how to rescue the godly from trial, and to keep the unrighteous under punishment until the day of judgment" (2 Pt 2:9).

Note that in the same breath that we ask not to be subjected to a trial, we ask the Lord to deliver us from all evil. We don't want the time of temptation, but if we find ourselves in it, we pray God will lead us through.

Just a few verses before the Our Father prayer, in Matthew chapter 4, Jesus enters the desert to be tempted. He experiences temptation to share this part of our humanity with us. As Christians, as children of God, we can then share with Jesus the rewards of the kingdom as well as the challenges of the cross.

We should see a time of trial with spiritual eyes and recognize the gravity of what is at stake. We have free will, which the Lord gave us, to make this choice for faithfulness or to abandon our faith. Jesus knows this and shares in our prayer to the Father that we might endure as he endured. As James writes: "Blessed is anyone who endures temptation (*peirasmos*). Such a one has stood the test and will receive the crown of life that the Lord has promised to those who love him" (Jas 1:12).

When we enter temptation, we do so as sons and daughters of God. We enter with Jesus and receive strength through the Holy Spirit, promised to us until the end of the age. As John writes in the Book of Revelation, "Because you have kept my word of patient endurance, I will keep you from the hour of trial (*peirasmos*) that is coming on the whole world to test the inhabitants of the earth" (3:10).

At the end of this great prayer that Jesus taught us, we ask to be spared from times of trial that make us doubt Our Lord, that weaken our faith, or that cause us to lose sight of our inheritance in Christ. We pray that in everything, God delivers us from the temptation or through it safely.

The Our Father is a prayer of sonship. It is a prayer whose every petition indicates a desire that we stay in union with the Father through his Son, Jesus. In the words that Jesus gave us, we recognize our adoption, asking to be made holy like him so his will on earth can be manifested in us. We are sustained through this union in Jesus, the Bread of Life, so we can pour out his forgiveness to others and withstand trial, never losing sight of our adoption as sons and daughters while here on earth.

Now that's a prayer. Praise be to God.

Reflect

REFLECTION FROM AN EARLY CHURCH FATHER

"And lead us not into temptation, O Lord. Is this then what the Lord teaches us to pray, that we may not be tempted at all? How then is it said elsewhere, 'a man untempted, is a man unproved; and again, My brethren, count it all joy when you fall into various temptations' (James 1:2)?

But does perchance the entering into temptation mean the being overwhelmed by the temptation? For temptation is, as it were, like a winter torrent difficult to cross. Those therefore who are not overwhelmed in temptations, pass through, showing themselves excellent swimmers, and not being swept away by them at all; while those who are not such, enter into them and are overwhelmed.

As for example, Judas having entered into the temptation of the love of money, swam not through it, but was overwhelmed and was strangled both in body and spirit. Peter entered into the temptation of the denial; but having entered, he was not overwhelmed by it, but manfully swam through it, and was delivered from the temptation. Listen again, in another place, to a company of unscathed saints, giving thanks for deliverance from temptation, you, O God hast proved us; you have tried us by fire like as silver is tried. You brought us into the net; you layed afflictions upon our loins. You have caused men to ride over our heads; we went through fire and water; and you brought us out into a place of rest. You see them speaking boldly in regard to their having passed through and not been pierced. But you brought us out into a place of rest; now their coming into a place of rest is their being delivered from temptation."

— Cyril of Jerusalem[2]

As you ponder these verses, journal your thoughts in the space provided. Reflect on the Scripture passage (and subsequent supporting passages) from "Read." Is there a word or phrase that especially stands out to you? What do these verses say to you? What is the Holy Spirit showing you in these Scripture passages?

TRIAL

Image: Convent of the Annunciation in Alba de Tormes, Spain, where Teresa died

Respond

In this section, we will review Teresa's response to God's word. May she serve as an example as you seek out how the Holy Spirit is prompting you to respond.

THE END OF THE WAY

Whereas Teresa was quick to brush off human resistance to her work, she was keenly aware and quite affected by the spiritual attacks of the Devil. In her new house, the Monastery of St. Joseph in Ávila, Teresa's work underwent tremendous spiritual attacks. She lightheartedly writes that the Spanish Inquisition gave her no fear. Her only fear was not hearing from the Lord, or that the Devil was deceiving her:

> Some persons came to me with great fear to tell me we were in trouble and that it could happen that others might accuse me of something and report me to the Inquisitors. This amused me and made me laugh, for I never had any fear of such a possibility. If anyone were to see that I went against the slightest ceremony of the Church in a matter of faith, I myself knew well that I would die a thousand deaths for the faith or for any truth of Sacred Scripture. And I said they shouldn't be afraid about these possible accusations; that it would be pretty bad for my soul if there were something in it of the sort that I should have to fear the Inquisition; that I thought that if I did have something to fear I'd go myself to seek out the Inquisitors: and that if I were accused, the Lord would free me, and I would be the one to gain.[3]

Teresa often wondered why the Devil cared about stopping the founding of the Monastery of St. Joseph. The determination of the Devil to thwart and distract Teresa speaks to the power of her prayer life and her reforms:

> I was startled by what the devil stirred up against a few poor little women and how everyone thought — I mean those opposed that this house would be so harmful to the city. There were only twelve women and the prioress (for there were to be no more); and they were living such a strict life. If the house were harmful or a mistake, it would be so for these women; but that it would be harmful to the city didn't make sense. But the adversaries found so many reasons for opposing it.[4]

In the latter years of her life, she continued to undergo trials as she founded more monasteries, with formidable spiritual attacks from the evil one. God was always faithful, however, in helping Teresa navigate the suffering — whether it was a temptation she needed to overcome or an experience that God was permitting — in order to further teach her.

Teresa, however, was insightful and shrewd. Anything the Devil did, she wrote down and analyzed, sharing it with her religious sisters and, ultimately, us. Teresa sought discernment of whether each experience of a trial was instruction from God or a spiritual attack from the enemy. It took her a lifetime to master this discernment, speaking with many priests and theologians:

> It is always good that we walk with fear and caution. For, although the work may be from God, the devil at times can transform himself into an angel of light; and if the soul has not a great deal of experience, it will not

> discern the devil's work — and, in fact, it must have so much experience that it needs to come close to the very summit of prayer in order to have such discernment.[5]

Her advice for discernment during a time of trial is unsurprising but wise: Turn to prayer:

> What I advise strongly is not to abandon prayer, for in prayer people will understand what they are doing and win repentance from the Lord and fortitude to lift themselves up. And you must believe that if you give up prayer, you are, in my opinion, courting danger.[6]

Teresa reminds us that because prayer is so powerful, the Devil is quite intent on leading a person to abandon it, whether through discouragement, false humility, busyness, or distraction. For Teresa, twenty years passed between her initial surrender to the Lord in religious life and the favors finally brought on by a deep life of prayer — a delay due to a false humility that she was unworthy to come before the Lord in prayer.

As Teresa spiritually advanced through her prayer life, she often willingly engaged in spiritual warfare, knowing that she would help those who were weaker in virtue. She would pray constantly for the souls of others and was even confronted by demons who had been cast away from the soul for which she was praying:

> There was no doubt, in my opinion, that they were afraid of me, for I remained so calm and so unafraid of them all. All the fears I usually felt left me even to this day. For although I sometimes saw them, as I shall relate afterward, I no longer had hardly any fear of them; rather it seemed they were afraid of me. I was left with a mastery over them truly given by the Lord of all; I pay no more attention to them than to flies.[7]

She reached the point where every moment of her day was spent in prayer; she felt Christ by her side and was never afraid. This closeness to Christ compelled her to write down what she knew and drove all her efforts for reform:

> I don't understand these fears, "The devil The devil!," when we can say "God! God," and make the devil tremble. Yes, for we already know that he cannot stir if the Lord doesn't permit him to. What is this? Without doubt, I fear those who have such great fear of the devil more than I do the devil himself, for he can't do anything to me. Whereas these others, especially if they are confessors, cause severe disturbance; I have undergone some years of such great trial that I am amazed now at how I was able to suffer it. Blessed be the Lord who has so truly helped me![8]

At the end of her book *The Way of Perfection*, Teresa concludes with a look at Matthew 6:13, discussing the desire not to be led into temptation but delivered from evil:

> The soldiers of Christ, those who experience contemplation and engage in prayer, are eager to fight. They never fear public enemies very much; they already recognize them and know that these enemies have no power against the strength the Lord gives and that they themselves always come out the victors and with much gain. They never turn from these enemies.
>
> Those whom they fear and it is right they fear and always ask the Lord to be freed from them are the traitorous enemies, the devils who transfigure themselves into angels of light, who come disguised.
>
> Not until they have done much harm to the soul do they allow themselves to be recognized. They suck away our blood and destroy our virtues, and we go about

> in the midst of the same temptation but do not know it. With regard to these enemies, daughters, let us ask and often beg the Lord in the Our Father to free us and not let us walk into temptation, so that they will not draw us into error or hide the light and truth from us, that the poison will be discovered. Oh, how rightly does our good Master ask this for us and teach us to ask for it.[9]

Teresa founded at least twelve more monasteries for the Discalced Carmelite Order before falling ill at the age of sixty-seven. Her last moments on earth were spent founding a new monastery in Burgos, Spain before passing away in the city of Alba de Tormes. Her last words were: "O my Lord and my Spouse, the hour that I have longed for has come. It is time to meet one another."

In 1970, Pope Paul VI named Teresa of Ávila as a "Doctor of the Church" — the first female saint so named — saying:

> Although she had repeatedly declared her inability to understand and teach, she was nevertheless able to understand, teach and write, inspired by God, on very profound subjects, considering Christ the only source of her doctrine and almost a living book... This doctrine excels a very deep sense of reality, an intimate understanding of the mystery of the living God, of Christ the Saviour and the Church, a living experience of grace, which raises and develops nature, adorned with so many gifts.[10]

On the prayer that Jesus taught, Teresa concludes:

> Certainly, it never entered my mind that this prayer contained so many deep secrets; for now you have seen the entire spiritual way contained in it, from the beginning stages until God engulfs the soul and gives it to drink abundantly from the fount of living water, which he said was to be found at the end of the way. And having come out of it — I mean of this prayer — I don't know how to go any further.[11]

These deep secrets are for every child of God, adopted into sonship through Christ Jesus. This simple prayer, which we often say so casually, becomes a foundation for detachment, humility, and love of neighbor, drawing us closer to resembling our holy Father. Like Teresa, may we never abandon the pursuit of a deep prayer life, one inviting in a love that "overwhelms reason." Teresa's lived example and written words encourage us never to cease praying until we fully unite with our loving Father in his eternal kingdom.

DISCUSSION QUESTIONS

1.Why did Teresa view opposition from others with little attention? Who was the real agitator?

2. What was Teresa's answer to fending off spiritual attacks? What makes you more vulnerable?

3.What legacy did Teresa leave behind?

4. Where do you place the blame when you suffer a trial? Is there a more appropriate source that you need to identify?

5. In what ways has your understanding of the Our Father prayer changed? How so?

6. What ways has this study encouraged you to change your prayer life? What has challenged you most?

Stay awake and pray that you may not come into the time of trial; the spirit is indeed willing, but the flesh is weak.

(MT 26:41)

Image: A painting of Teresa's death by Giovanni Segala

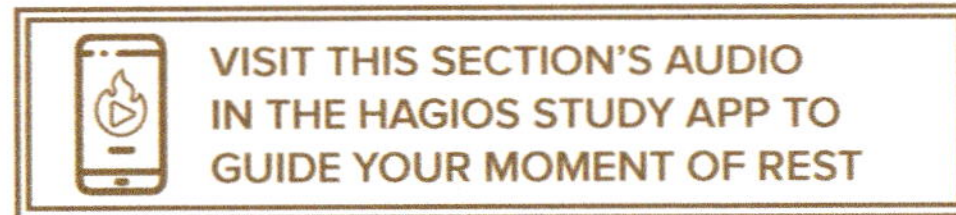

Below are Teresa's final reflections on the Our Father in her book *The Way of Perfection*. Use these words for your time of prayer as you continue on your earthly journey toward heaven. As you finish this study, visit the Hagios Study mobile app for this section's Rest meditation song to assist you in your time with the Lord.

DELIVER ME, LORD

Deliver me, Lord, from this shadow of death, deliver me from so many trials, deliver me from so many sufferings, deliver me from so many changes, from so many compliments that we are forced to receive while still living, from so many, many, many things that tire and weary me, that would tire anyone reading this if I mentioned them all …

O my Lord and my God, deliver me now from all evil and be pleased to bring me to the place where all blessings are. What do they still hope for here, those to whom You have given knowledge of what the world is, and those who have a living faith concerning what the Eternal Father has kept for them?[12]

INTRODUCTION

1. Teresa of Ávila, *The Way of Perfection*, in *The Collected Works of Saint Teresa of Avila*, Volume 2, trans. Kieran Kavanaugh, O.C.D. and Otilio Rodriguez, O.C.D (ICS, 2017), 202.

2. Ibid., 53–54.

WEEK 1

1. "Kryptos," *Blue Letter Bible*, blueletterbible.org/lexicon/g2927/lxx/lxx/0-1/.

2. "Apodidōmi," *Blue Letter Bible*, blueletterbible.org/lexicon/g591/lxx/lxx/0-1/.

3. John Chrysostom, *Homilies on the Gospel of Saint Matthew: Homily XIX*, in *Nicene and Post-Nicene Fathers, First Series*, vol. 10, ed. Philip Schaff (New York, 1888), 133.

4. Cyril of Alexandria, *Homily LXX*, in *Commentary on the Gospel of Luke*, ed. R. Payne Smith (1859), 359.

5. Kieran Kavanaugh, O.C.D. "The Book of Her Life — Introduction," in *The Collected Works of Saint Teresa of Avila*, Volume 1, trans. Kieran Kavanaugh, O.C.D. and Otilio Rodriguez, O.C.D.0 (ICS, 2017), 34.

6. Teresa of Ávila, *The Book of Her Life*, in *The Collected Works of Saint Teresa of Avila*, Volume 1, 96.

7. Teresa of Ávila, *Interior Castle*, in *The Collected Works of Saint Teresa of Avila*, Volume 2, 427.

8. Teresa of Ávila, *The Book of Her Life*, 223.

9. Ibid., 219.

10. Ibid., 243.

11. Teresa of Ávila, *The Way of Perfection*, 129.

12. Teresa of Ávila, "Seeking God," in *The Collected Works of Saint Teresa of Avila*, Volume 3, trans. Kieran Kavanaugh, O.C.D. and Otilio Rodriguez, O.C.D (ICS, 2017), 527.0

WEEK 2

1. Or verse 7, depending on translation.

2. "Patēr," *Blue Letter Bible*, blueletterbible.org/lexicon/g3962/lxx/lxx/0-1/.

3. Or verse 7, depending on translation.

4. "Hagiazō," *Blue Letter Bible*, blueletterbible.org/lexicon/g37/lxx/lxx/0-1/.

5. Chrysostom, *Homily XIX*, 134.

6. Teresa of Ávila, *The Book of Her Life*, 54.

7. Ibid., 55.

8. Ibid., 60.

9. Ibid., 64.

10. Ibid., 64.

11. Teresa of Ávila, *The Way of Perfection*, 137.

12. Ibid., 143.

13. Ibid., 129.

14. Ibid., 139.

15. Teresa of Ávila, "In the Hands of God," in *The Collected Works of Saint Teresa of Avila*, Volume 3, 515.

WEEK 3

1. "Basileia," *Blue Letter Bible*, blueletterbible.org/lexicon/g932/kjv/tr/0-1/.

2. "Thelēma," *Blue Letter Bible*, blueletterbible.org/lexicon/g2307/lxx/lxx/0-1/.

3. Cyprian of Carthage. *Treatise 4: On the Lord's Prayer*, in *Ante-Nicene Fathers*, vol. 5, ed. Alexander Roberts, James Donaldson, and A. Cleveland Coxe (New York, 1886), 451.

4. Augustine of Hippo. *On the Sermon on the Mount*, bk. 2, chap. 11, in *Nicene and Post-Nicene Fathers*, First Series, vol. 6, ed. Philip Schaff (New York, 1888), 40.

5. Teresa of Ávila, *The Book of Her Life*, 70.

6. Ibid., 72.

7. Ibid., 82.

8. Ibid., 96.

9. Teresa of Ávila, *The Way of Perfection*, 150.

10. Ibid., 160.

11. Teresa of Ávila, *The Book of Her Life*, 202.

12. Teresa of Ávila, *The Way of Perfection*, 163.

WEEK 4

1. "Epiousios," *Blue Letter Bible*, blueletterbible.org /lexicon/g1967/kjv/tr/0-1/.

2. "Artos," *Blue Letter Bible*, blueletterbible.org/lexicon /g740/lxx/lxx/0-1/.

3. Cyprian of Carthage. *Treatise 4*: *On the Lord's Prayer*, 452.

4. Teresa of Ávila, *The Book of Her Life*, 168.

5. Ibid., 211.

6. Ibid., 228.

7. Ibid., 232, 246.

8. Ibid., 252.

9. Teresa of Ávila, *The Way of Perfection*, 169.

10. Ibid., 183.

WEEK 5

1. "Aphiēmi," *Blue Letter Bible*, blueletterbible.org/lexicon/ g863/lxx/lxx/0-1/.

2. Cyprian of Carthage, *Treatise 4*: On the Lord's Prayer, 453–454.

3. Teresa of Ávila, *The Book of Her Life*, 280.

4. Ibid., 168.

5. Ibid., .

6. Ibid., 206.

7. Ibid., 269.

8. Ibid., 281.

9. Ibid., 285.

10. Ibid., 289, 311.

11. Teresa of Ávila, *The Way of Perfection*, 180.

WEEK 6

1. "Peirasmos," *Blue Letter Bible*, blueletterbible.org/ lexicon/g3986/lxx/lxx/0-1/.

2. St. Cyril of Jerusalem, *On the Mysteries*: V, in *Nicene and Post-Nicene Fathers*, Second Series, vol. 7, ed. Philip Schaff and Henry Wace (New York, 1894), 155.

3. Teresa of Ávila, *The Book of Her Life*, 286.

4. Ibid., 318.

5. Ibid., 136.

6. Ibid., 140.

7. Ibid., 222.

8. Ibid., 223.

9. Teresa of Ávila, *The Way of Perfection*, 185.

10. Paul VI, *Multiformis Sapientia Dei*, Vatican.va.

11. Teresa of Ávila, *The Way of Perfection*, 202.

12. Ibid., 201–202.

IMAGE CREDITS

p 58: Elena F D, Public domain, via Wikimedia Commons

p 74: Zarateman, CC0, via Wikimedia Commons

p 82: https://www.flickr.com/photos/emeryjl/, CC BY 2.0 <https://creativecommons.org/licenses/by/2.0>, via Wikimedia Commons

p 84: https://www.flickr.com/photos/emeryjl/, CC BY 2.0 <https://creativecommons.org/licenses/by/2.0>, via Wikimedia Commons

p 100: Fallaner, CC BY-SA 4.0 <https://creativecommons.org/licenses/by-sa/4.0>, via Wikimedia Commons

p 106: Luis Rogelio HM, CC BY-SA 2.0 <https://creativecommons.org/licenses/by-sa/2.0>, via Wikimedia Commons

Reflect Notes

Reflect Notes

Reflect Notes

Reflect Notes